Travels in Portland

~~mmm~~Arrived late today and my
cousin picked us up at the airport.
After cozying up at ~~their~~ place,
we slept great & were ready for
the next days adventures.

Mt Hood - the ~~Fuji~~-like volcano that
overlooks Portland -
skiing, hiking -
just a huge presense.

We hit the highlights of the Columbia
River Gorge. Cousin Mike says it's
known for it's hikes, rare flowers, views.
Then on to the Coast - Cannon Beach.
So close to the city -
beach walks, sunsets.

Finally -- time to relax. Went to Caffe
Mingo. It's a small, Local, family-like
restaurant. The waiters ~~interacting~~
giving us info on the wine, local area.
So casual & comforting. ~~Food~~
~~was~~ Nonna-inspired. I'll be meeting
one of the waiters tomorrow
for a hike in
Forest Park.
He's way good-looking so hopefully !

m
CAFFE MINGO

807 NW 21st Avenue, Portland, Oregon 97209  503.226.4646

# Take it slowly

Lavazza, **partner of Slow Food,** expresses its love of flavour and its passion for coffee in the epitomising phrase: Take It Slowly. This expression is inspired by Slow Food's fundamental philosophy that the best way to savour the finest things in life is to take them slowly. Slow Food is an association, which is devoted to those who expect the highest quality and appreciate the finest taste sensations.

**ITALY'S FAVOURITE COFFEE**

Magazine of the International Slow Food Movement

**Editor and publisher**
Carlo Petrini

**Director**
Alberto Capatti

**Art director**
Dante Albieri

**Editor-in-chief**
Giovanni Ruffa

**Editorial staff**
Alessandro Barosi, Giovanni Bellingeri, Roberto Burdese,
Barbara Carrara, Paolo Di Croce, John Irving, Roberta Lovera,
Raffaella Ponzio, Cinzia Scaffidi

**Editorial secretary**
Elena Marino

**Editor of the English edition**
Giles Watson

**Editors of the German edition**
Luigi Wanner, Carla Barzanò

**Editor of the French edition**
Eve-Marie Zizza

**Production**
Maria Vittoria Negro

**Layout**
Stefano Pallaro

**Translations**
Elke Barent, Juan Bureo, Daniele Dell'Agli, Christina Dubbers,
Anya Fernald, Cecilia Gaggini, Ute Ludwig Garetto, Elena
Giovanelli, Miriam Maimouni, Catherine Mas, Davide Panzieri,
Ronnie Richards, Paloma Rodriguez, Ailsa Wood

**Cover**
photo Larry Towell, Magnum/Contrasto

**Slow Food Editore**
via della Mendicità Istruita, 45 - 12042 Bra (Cn) Italy
tel. ++39 0172 419611  fax ++39 0172 411218
e-mail: slowinfo@slowfood.com
web site: www.slowfood.com

Registrazione Tribunale di Alba (Cn) al numero 2/96
direttore responsabile Giovanni Ruffa

Slow Food® Editore

**One issue**
Italy 6,5 Euro;
Europe 9,5 Euro;
United States of America and Canada 14 US$;
Central and South America, Asia, Africa, Oceania 16.95 US$
Australian bookstores 18 AUD

**Annual subscription**
Italy (10 issues) 50 Euro;
Europe (5 issues) 40 Euro;
United States of America and Canada (5 issues) 50 US$;
Central and South America, Asia, Africa, Oceania (5 issues) 60 US$

**ISBN** 88-8499-022-X

**Print**
L'Artistica - Savigliano (Cn)

**Photo-offset lithography**
Ponti - Boves (Cn)

**Editorial offices**
via della Mendicità Istruita, 45 - Bra
tel. ++39 0172 419611  fax ++39 0172 411218

**Administration**
via della Mendicità Istruita, 14 - Bra
tel. ++39 0172 419611  fax ++39 0172 421293
c.c.p. 17519125

**Advertising**
Slow Food Promozione
Ivan Piasentin, Olivia Reviglio, Enrico Bonura
via della Mendicità Istruita, 14 - Bra
tel. ++39 0172 419611  fax ++39 0172 413640
e-mail: o.reviglio@slowfood.it

For France
Slow Food France - Charlotte Paressant
via della Mendicità Istruita, 14 - Bra
tel. ++39 0172 419650  fax ++39 0172 421293
e-mail: charlotte@slowfood.it

For Germany
Slow Food Deutschland e.V.
Geiststraße, 81 - Münster
tel. / fax ++49 0 251 793368
e-mail: info@slowfood.de

For Switzerland
Slow Food Schweiz - Susanne Zweidler
Dufourstrasse 187, CH-8008 Zürich
tel. ++41 1 3803949  fax ++41 1 3802990
e-mail: info@slowfood.ch

For United States of America
Slow Food USA - Patrick Martins
PO BOX 1737 - New York NY 10021
tel. ++1 212 9655640 fax ++1 212 2260672
e-mail: patrick@slowfoodusa.org

For UK
Wendy Fogarty
The Forager Ltd
Tel. / fax ++44 0 1844 339 362
Mobile: ++44 0 7712 842 777
e-mail: wfogarty@compuserve.com

Slow Food Greece
tel. ++30 (0) 19221173

**Issue closed**
15-12-2001

Pages: Bioprima Book paper, cover: Fabria card from the Mi-
liani Fabriano mills.
This paper is made of excellent chlorine-free cellulose (TCF). This
ecological paper does not contain any optical beaching, it is acid-
free with alkaline reservation, which guarantees long resistance.

Periodical postage is paid at Rahway, N.J.
Slow (ISSN awaiting registration) is published in february, may,
august, november by Slow Food Arcigola Editore srl.
Subscription price is $ 44 per year. POSTMASTER send address
corrections to IMX America International, c/o Mercury Airfreight
Intl. 2323 Randolph Ave, avenel, NJ 07001

www.slowfood.com

# Authors

Alessandra Abbona ITALY, **Carlo Bogliotti** ITALY, **Nicola Ferrero** ITALY, **Paolo Di Croce** ITALY, **Annette Frei Berthould** SWITZERLAND, Corby Kummer USA, **Alessandro Monchiero** ITALY, **Vítor Neto** PORTUGAL, **Claire Panzer** SWITZERLAND, **Carlo Petrini** ITALY, **Maria José Ritta** PORTUGAL, **Stefano Sardo** ITALY, **Cinzia Scaffidi** ITALY, **Vandana Shiva** INDIA

**Photographs of the Slow Food Award at Oporto are by Tim Turner**

**Thanks to** Mariame Balde, Ernesto Barrera, Vinod Kumar Bhatt, Giorgio and Alicia De Angeli, Ahmed El Amrani, Joaquim Figueiredo, Toni Gomiscek, Instituto de Cultura de Tabasco, Kim Chin Wha, Kim Jong Duk, M'Hamed Koutari (Ministère des Eaux et Forêts du Maroc), Virginia Kristensen, Frank Marciano, Vishnu Mohan, Joao Navalho, Robin Rae, Maithé Relecom, Rosa María Romo López, Ailyn Tan, Mario Tapia, Gerardo Vásquez Lugo, Dejan Zagorac

**Carlo Petrini**

**Maria José Ritta**

**Vítor Neto**

**Cinzia Scaffidi**

Africa, Republic of South Africa, Irene

America, Argentina, Coronel Moldes, Province of Sal

**Europe, Portugal, Ria Formosa National Park, Algarve**

Europe, Serbia, Mionica

**Vandana Shiva**

**Africa, Morocco, Tamanar**

America, Mexico, Tabasco, Comalcalco

**America, Peru, Cuzco**

Asia, India, Dehra Dun, Uttar Anchal

Europe, Switzerland, Geneva

**Paolo Di Croce**

America, Peru, Puno

**Europe, Turkey, Anatolia, Ismailk**

Africa, Guinea, Futah Djallon

America, Chile, Santiago

Asia, South Korea, Jijuk-Ri, Namhae Kun

# Contents

# Oporto, 13 October 2001

Carlo
Petrini
President
of Slow
Food

This issue of *Slow* is entirely dedicated to the 2001 edition of the Slow Food Award held last year on 13 October at the monastery of Sâo Bento in Oporto. These pages will report on the second phase of a great cultural project aimed at discovering, revealing and promoting natural heritage and life, in all its many facets, and the identities of the 14 deserving recipients whose efforts have earned this reward. Theirs are exemplary experiences, stories of men and women working to defend biodiversity on our planet. We wanted to introduce them as instructive examples, capable of explaining better than any words what the Award means, and what strength and direction it will have in the future. We have organized the articles into three basic themes; three lines of thought that bind the winners and their activities together. The first is **biodiversity**, a subject that is, of course, common to all the Award winners. Yet it is particularly dear to Noel Honeyborne from South Africa, Carlos Lewis from Argentina, Predrag Petrovic from Serbia, and Joao Navalho and Victor Verdello from Portugal. This section

is preceded by an interview with José Esquinas-Alcázar, Secretary of the FAO Commission on Genetic Resources for Food and Agriculture. Involved with this subject for decades, Esquinas-Alcázar received a special honor from Slow Food in Oporto. The second group of stories involves only **women**; courageous, capable women who, from Switzerland to Morocco, Mexico to Peru and India, have shown - some by building agricultural cooperatives, others by revitalizing communities and local cultures, or rescuing of long abandoned resources - that it is possible to overcome marginalization and ancient subjugation to become the main players in exciting projects. Finally, the third theme is of the recovery of **native cultures** along with the knowledge connected to them. We have observed this is noble process in Peru, Turkey, Guinea, Chile, and South Korea, along with the recovery of traditional farming methods, the rediscovery of forgotten foods and the continuance of ancestral work practices. The feeling I had in Oporto, before an audience with representatives of almost every country, their diversity imprinted on their faces and pro-

*Carlo Petrini and José Esquinas-Alcazar*

claimed by their languages and dress, will remain indelible in my memory. At the monastery of Sâo Bento, I physically touched what Slow Food is becoming: a melting pot of cultures, geographically distant but close in their common ideals and intentions. First and foremost of those aims is the restoration of dignity and motivation to farmers, who are the real custodians of traditional, local flavors and so also of biodiversity and the balance of ecosystems. Promoting the value of work in the countryside is the task I want to point out to the new gourmet, whose emergence Slow Food aspires to encourage, a foodlover capable of combining the search for sensory pleasure with a new sense of responsibili-

ty and of uniting the awareness of products with knowledge of their human history. Today, it is no longer possible or just to wish to passively benefit from agricultural, food and wine resources while refusing to find out about where they come from, what gives them their existence and what fruits they yield, or to communicate with those who ensure their supply. Without a sense of responsibility toward our heritage of food and cooking, as well as its future users, and without the awareness of the ethical choices this heritage imposes on us, there can be no future. The paradox of sensory pleasure today lies precisely in the discipline demanded by its pursuit, and the variety of manifestations it can assume.

For most of the 20th century, excellence in the realm of taste brought with it the hegemony of certain culinary, commercial and production models, embodied, at least in Western culture, in French gastronomy, the decline of gustatory imperialism, and the rejection of agricultural and alimentary standardization. This imposed the redefinition of roles and strategies and the acceptance of diversity as the guiding principle of a quality-oriented effort that cannot be realized without a new agriculture founded on local resources, on knowledge and skill, and on respect for the environment. Now moving toward its third edition, the Slow Food Award is the testing ground for that future.

# In praise of identity

Maria José
Ritta
Presidency
of the
Portuguese
Republic

Slow Food, the name of the international Association that promotes this magazine emblematically sums up the attitude many people have towards good food, time and their fellow human beings.

The attitude is essentially part of a culture, and a cultural heritage, in which emotional relationships with things and people merge with individual lifestyle habits. One might

say that this is a real culture of resistance, since the current trend is towards instantly consumable pragmatism, as if eating, drinking and socializing were exclusively governed by the quantity of protein assimilated and the frenetic rhythm of time ticking by.

As I said at the 2001 Slow Food Award, the idea of holding this ceremony in Oporto during the year in which it is, with Rotterdam, the European Capital of Culture, could not have been more appropriate. The granite strength of this old harbor and the rich humanity of its people entitle us to feel that the identity of peoples and places is not destined to disappear into the maw of dominant cultural models and stereotypes.

In places like Oporto, eating and drinking still provide opportunities to look at the world and our fellows with the respect they deserve. For many people here, sitting at table together is a celebration of the pleasures of life and the relationships it embraces, a simple but effective ritual against loneliness and the dehumanization of daily life. I hope the international Slow Food Movement will continue to expand its activities and find in Portugal appropriate reasons and examples to promote its ideas. Slow Food will always be welcome here.

*Lisbon, 9 November 2001*

# A cultural heritage

*Vítor Neto
Portuguese
Secretary
of
State
for
Tourism*

The city of Oporto, European Capital of Culture 2001, was the host venue for the 2nd Slow Food Award. This event was hugely successful and enabled many people to realize the important role played by the international Slow Food Movement, which carries out much valuable work for the protection and preservation of the values of traditional cuisine. These values are founded on genuine farm products and the safeguarding of biodiversity, two factors that fully justify the support of this event by the Ministry of Finance, through the Secretary of State for Tourism.

Good food reflects the path followed by peoples as their civilizations evolved and is the focus of increasing attention. This growing interest has led to the launching of projects of various kinds and intense publishing activity. If we look beyond the material signs left by every culture and age, we see that everyday food-related habits are at least as important as those signs. They combine with geographical, climatic, historical and reli-gious elements that give them their specific nature. They are an integral part of a people's identity, and throw light on its history.

It is therefore a privilege for Portugal to have been chosen to host this event, which in a sense mirrors the plan of action defined by the Portuguese government in this sector. Portugal can boast a rich and våried cuisine. It is one of our most authentic and remarkable cultural manifestations, a heritage which must be preserved and promoted at all costs. In addition, it has undeniable value as a driving force for the tourist industry.

The Portuguese government, fully aware of this heritage and its importance in cultural, financial, tourism and rural development terms, has taken an initiative we believe is groundbreaking. Resolution no.96/2000 of the Council of Ministers, dated 26 July, recognizes food and drink as an intangible asset and part of the country's cultural heritage. Moreover a work group has been created, with representatives from a vast range of public and private bodies, whose mission is

*Joao Navalho and Vítor Neto*

to develop a series of activities to protect and promote the national heritage of food and drink.

The lines of intervention start essentially from the study and promotions of Portuguese food and drink, highlighting the aspects that make it typical and distinctive, to the creation and management of a database of traditional Portuguese products and recipes. This is one of the most important aspects of the project because it will make information available to the public through a dedicated website. The second aspect is the organization of competitions to preserve and promote Portugal's food heritage, and encourage the creation of new recipes from traditional products.

It is equally important to underline aspects related to the promotion of our food heritage in the domestic market, where the main aim will be to qualify and differentiate the mark with food professionals, consumers, the general public and the country's schoolchildren, as well as in non-domestic markets, where mechanisms must be put in place to encourage food-related initiatives. The 'gastronomic' element of tourism packages can thus also be promoted, which will add value to our tourism product and differentiate Portugal's image in the international marketplace.

I would like to conclude by congratulating the international Slow Food Movement on its work, and in particular for this important event. My felicitations go also to all those from around the world who have taken part, especially the award winners – one of them from Portugal – and all the candidates and members of the Jury. I wish everyone every success in the future.

*Oporto, 13 October 2001*

# José's seeds

*C i n z i a   S c a f f i d i*

*Interview with José Esquinas-Alcázar, Secretary of the FAO Commission
on Genetic Resources for Food and Agriculture*

J osé Esquinas-Alcázar and Slow Food met in November 1996 at
the first Hall of Taste in Turin. Esquinas was there to speak at
the meeting to launch the Ark project. Little more than five
years have passed since then, a relatively brief period during which
our Movement and the Secretary of the FAO Commission on Genetic
Resources for Food and Agriculture have found more and more opportunities to meet, collaborate and share common views. When the
Honorary Committee of the Slow Food Award for Biodiversity was
created in 2000, it seemed perfectly natural to invite Esquinas to participate. At the second edition of the Award in Oporto, Esquinas received an Honorary Award which read:

*For having dedicated his entire professional life and intellectual re-
sources to applied and scientific research concerning genetic resources to be utilized in agriculture, working in his field of expertise
at the FAO to help promote the protection of biodiversity as an important value in every corner of the globe. For having always looked
with interest to new ideas and opportunities for collaboration with
other bodies and organizations, ever ready to accept different methods of operating. For having been one of the main actors in raising
international consciousness on the subject of genetic erosion and the
need for safeguarding the biogenetic heritage of the planet through
government regulation and changes in the behavior of the general
population.*

When we say 'his entire professional life', we are not alluding generical-
ly to his work. The world of genetics was his main interest from the
very start.

*Peshawar, Pakistan, Photo Roger Wood, Corbis/Grazia Neri*

*How did your enthusiasm for this field of research begin?*

That is a fairly long and complicated story. I was born in Spain, in La Mancha. My parents had a farm of about 50 hectares planted to wheat, olives and vines. The family had been farmers for many generations. Though we children – I have a brother and two sisters – went to school, during summer vacations we all had to work in the countryside. My father felt it was very important and, besides, we liked it. Mostly, we helped with the grain harvest. We started before dawn and worked until sundown. Everyone had their own special job, which changed depending on our age. We all participated, young and old, working alongside seasonal workers. Back then, the wheat was harvested by hand and every summer the Andaluses would arrive, professional harvesters that started from the south of Spain, where the wheat ripened first, and traveled in teams all summer, gradually moving further north.

I learned many things during those years. In some ways, more than I ever learned at university. When I had to choose a faculty, my dream was to study medicine. Then, for various reasons including cost and the time necessary, I decided to enroll in Agriculture, which in Spain is part of the Polytechnic. But after I graduated and I was choosing a topic for my first doctorate, I went back to my first love, in a certain sense, and opted for genetics.

*But not everyone takes the step from genetics to the defense of biodiversity. In fact, you could have gone off in a completely different direction.*

That is true but... it was the melons that saved me. I chose a field research project that involved collecting all the varieties of melons present in Spain at the time. I had a very small grant so I had to make a virtue of necessity. I wrote to elementary school teachers, mayors and captains of the Guardia Civil, asking them all to send me seeds from the melons in their towns and villages. I took many trips around Spain, always looking for seeds, and some of these were enlightening. The Ministry of Agriculture gave us the use of a plot of land for experimental cultivation and for a few years, I worked there with many students, from medicine as well as agriculture, who volunteered to help this research. In the end, we collected 357 varieties. We planted 16 specimens of each and analyzed around 60 parameters for each fruit, an enormous but fascinating task. That was in 1970. I am sure that if I were to try to put together the same collection again, I could no longer find 90 percent of those varieties. Spain is presently the largest producer of melons in Europe and six or seven varieties cover the entire market. Those grown by farmers to satisfy the needs of the family have been sacrificed for varieties that can be more easily sold.

At any rate, this research, along with the work on my family's farm, is part of the reason for my interest in the world of farming. I had this direct contact with farmers and began to think that all their knowledge was neither being preserved nor respected.

*You said that some of your trips were enlightening. Was this from the human or scientific standpoint?*
From the human point of view, the entire experience was very important. But one trip in particular and a chance meeting helped me to immediately understand the heart of the problem that would occupy me for the next 30 years.

Out of a cabinet, Esquinas-Alcázar pulls a hefty envelope containing enlargements of color photographs.
One of them is of a short, old man not much taller than his donkey. Leaning on his cane, he stares at the lens with severe eyes that shine from underneath the brim of a black hat.
Something is in his mouth, maybe a cigarette, maybe a piece of wood. He seems held together by his dark clothes but his hands, knotted as roots, betray his physical strength.

*Naukluft Park, Namibia, Photo Nige J Dennis, Corbis/Grazia Neri Urgantch, Uzbekistan, Photo Marc Garanger, Corbis/Grazia Neri*

You see this farmer? I don't even know what his name was and have no idea whether or not he is still alive. I took this picture purely by chance, almost to thank him for the time he had dedicated to me. He appeared in front of me on his donkey during one of my seed collecting trips. I was waiting for a bus in an isolated area then he showed up and asked me what I was doing. With all the enthusiasm of my 25 years, I started telling him the whole story, about the seeds and the danger of extinction, but he stopped me. He had already understood it all and said, "Even if a disease comes along that kills all the melons, mine will still be here. I have a kind that never gets diseases". I asked him if I could have some seeds and he said, "Sure, it's near here". 'Near here' meant a three and a half-hour ride with him on his donkey but in the end I got the seeds. Anyway, later, when they were analyzed, they turned out to be resistant to a particular type of *fusarium* fungus. It was those seeds that became the basis for creating resistance to that type of fungal disease for many melon producers around the world. And no one has ever thanked him. I wouldn't even know how to get back in touch with him. No one ever worries about rewarding, financially or morally, those who had the intelligence and farsightedness to preserve their seeds.

*This is one of the fundamental points in the international treaty on phytogenetic resources for food and agriculture, approved by the FAO in November.*

Exactly. I consider this treaty a real milestone. It is the first international treaty of the millennium. We worked for so many years, fine-tuning and discussing every word, and finally it was approved by every country in the world with only two abstentions (the US and Japan) and no votes against.

*What will this treaty accomplish?*

There are three fundamental points to the agreement. First and foremost, the conservation of genetic diversity becomes the legal duty of national governments. This means it is not just a declaration of intent or theoretical approval of the concept. Signatory governments must pass legislation to observe this commitment, especially for future generations. Second, the treaty aims for broader and more sustainable use of genetic resources. Finally, there is, for the first time, a declaration the distribution of benefits deriving from the use of phytogenetic resources must be fair and equitable. This protects the interests of farmers, who are included in this last point. Never before had farmers even been taken into consideration.

If it is true that genetic resources are a treasure, then we must ask ourselves who are the treasurers. Those who have protected them up till now or those who can afford facilities to preserve them, such as large germ plasma banks? I believe the world owes a debt to those farmers who use traditional agricultural systems, particularly in less developed areas.

*Morocco. Photo Jamie Harrow,*
*Corbis/Grazia Neri*
*Kalahari, South Africa. Photos*
*Anthony Bannister, Corbis/Grazia Neri*

*And what will happen now that the treaty has been approved?*
The treaty has been approved by the countries that belong to the FAO, in other words almost every country in the world. Now each individual government must ratify the agreement, which will go into force as soon as 40 countries have done so.

*Could the governments of those countries that abstained also refuse to ratify the agreement?*
In theory, even the governments of the countries that voted for it could refuse to ratify it. But this is an international agreement and the positions expressed at FAO headquarters are rarely contradicted by individual governments. The problem of ratification is also formal. For a regulation to be considered in force within a national territory, a country must approve it in its representative body, and logically this is not the FAO.

*Why did this treaty take so much time and effort, and how did you get from melons to the FAO?*

This is another very long story. As I said, in 1970 I was in Spain with my melons and my students. But in the meantime, other things had changed. It was the Franco period and, having finished my doctorate, I took advantage of a grant to study in the United States. At Davis, in California, I continued my research on melons but this time in the laboratory. This meant that, whereas before we studied the differences in varieties cultivated experimentally and then recorded data along with the agricultural and morphological differences of individual plants, now observations were done from the enzymatic point of view using electrophoresis. This method calculated the genetic distances between the different populations to reconstruct the phylogenetic tree of the species *Cucumis melo*, and then the genus *Cucumis*. This way, the paths were identified that the varieties had taken to arrive at their present site. Spanish melons were discovered to have arrived mostly from India and the Middle East. On Franco's death, I returned to Spain and teaching at the University of Madrid. In 1978, I took a six-month leave of absence because the FAO had accepted an application I had made almost a year earlier for a position in a project involving genetic resources.

*Why just six months?*

Because it was supposed to be for a limited time, leading up to the 1979 FAO conference. In fact, I am still here, and still on a leave of absence! The story of the treaty approved in November substantially coincides with my own career at the FAO.

*Do you mean to say that a project you thought would end in six months instead took 22 years of work?*

It isn't quite like that, although it is in a way. The truth is that many things have changed over the past few years and awareness has increased. For the 1979 conference – FAO conferences are held in odd-numbered years – I prepared a proposal for an international germ plasma bank and convention that was presented by the Spanish delegation presiding over the conference. Unfortunately however, and despite the support of many other delegations, mainly Latin American, it was not presented as a draft resolution, which would have allowed it to continue. I was very disappointed but decided to persevere. I began to hold informal meetings, working in the shadows, to try and spread awareness of the genetic resource issue, in part through the media.

*Sinkiang Uighur, China, Photo Galen Rowell, Corbis/Grazia Neri*

*What is an international germ plasma bank?*

I intentionally left this element vague in the project. It could be a real bank, created with the support of all participating countries, or it could simply be a case where the national germ plasma banks of individual governments are placed under the direction or jurisdiction of the FAO, and are therefore available to everyone. Many countries have one: Italy's is in Bari. At the 1981 conference, the 1977 Group of developing countries presented the project again at the FAO conference and a feasibility study was ordered. The study declared the project unworkable. Another door closed.

*More years of work lost?*

At the time, I really thought we had another two years, in other words until the next FAO conference, to try and get the project passed. So that meant another two years' hard labor. But then in 1983, came the first turning point. Spain offered to put its national bank under FAO jurisdiction to unblock the situation. And in November, an agreement was approved at the two-yearly conference. It was not binding on governments – this is the great difference with the present treaty – and was not approved unanimously for there were eight votes against from industrialized countries. On the same occasion, the request was made for the creation of a commission to monitor genetic resources. It was a very lively conference and in the end the FAO Commission on Phytogenetic Resources was created; it is now the Commission on Genetic Resources for Food and Agriculture.

*And you were nominated director of the Commission?*

Not right away. In the sense that at that point I tendered my resignation, having brought to an end the project begun five years earlier. But the director general rejected it, proposing that I become the Secretary of the Commission and start work right away on improving the international compromise that had just been approved. With analysis and the passage of time, that document has been expanded with annexes and parallel agreements, particularly one on the rights of farmers. Then came the 1992 Conference in Rio de Janeiro, with the Convention on Biological Diversity that become operative in 1993. At this point, the FAO asked to renegotiate the agreement and particularly to make it mandatory for governments. This was a great advance in quality. In fact, it led to seven years of negotiations among the various national governments until the present agreement was reached, containing the three objectives I mentioned before and which puts the emphasis on the rights of farmers.

*When do you think this question can be considered well and truly closed? In other words, when will the individual countries begin seriously to work in the direction indicated in the agreement?*

The ratification period could be lengthy. There is no deadline. This is partly because the FAO has no powers to impose a deadline. What has been decided is for the first 40 ratifications to be made as quickly as possible so the treaty will become completely operative, preferably before the food summit planned for June 2002. I believe our greatest difficulties will be in the initial phase. Then once the first countries ratify it, the others will soon follow, partly to avoid still being outside the treaty when the first meeting is held of the governing body, comprising the group of countries that have ratified the treaty. The governing body will develop the mechanisms to enable application of the treaty itself. However, some things are already moving. For example, in August 2001, the Indian Parliament passed the first laws on the rights of farmers.

*The first Indian law?*

No, the first law ever passed anywhere in the world specifically to safeguard the rights of farmers regarding genetic resources.

*Belize. Photo Kevin Schafer, Corbis/Grazia Neri*
*Kgaladi, South Africa. Photo Nigel J Dennis, Corbis/Grazia Neri*

# Noel Honeyborne

**N**oel Honeyborne, born in Alicedale, South Africa in 1946, studied electrical engineering before switching to animal husbandry and becoming a poultry expert. Since 1992, he has been working as Chief Research Technologist at the ARC (Agricultural Research Council) in Irene. His work with native poultry breeds has led to the Fowls for Africa project, which neatly links the task of saving old breeds with the fight against hunger in southern Africa. Fowls for Africa, founded in 1994, aims to make poultry production possible for small farmers, women and disadvantaged communities.

**Africa, Republic of South Africa, Irene**

### Native breeds

How did Noel Honeyborne come to specialize in poultry? "Producing meat from poultry", he explains, "is much faster than producing mutton, beef or pork. Poultry and eggs are easy to digest affordable, even for the very poor".

The demand for animal protein in South Africa has led to intensive poultry farming for fast food, at the same time causing a reduction in native and adapted breeds. Although many of these birds grow more slowly, they are good layers, have genes adapted to survival in extreme conditions, are less choosy about what they eat and more resistant to disease. Their meat has flavor and good texture. Four older breeds and one modern chicken were compared at a tasting. The modern

bird was white and juicy, but also somewhat tasteless and too soft on the palate. The others had darker meat and were a little tougher to chew but had much more flavor. These properties, acquired over hundreds of years, are important for breeding in the future and should be conserved. Honeyborne's institute sends thousands of chicks each year to the various provinces of South Africa and to other African countries. There are always indigenous birds among the chicks that are sent. Thanks to them, it has been possible to re-establish the poultry population following the devastation caused by New Castle disease. Re-introducing resistant, prolific, adaptable breeds plays an important part in ensuring nourishment for all. Keeping farmyard animals also gives women, in particular, the chance of making a living for themselves and their children.

Essentially, there are seven breeds – Black Australorp, New Hampshire, Rhode Island Red, Potchefstroom Koekoek, Ovambo, Venda and Naked Neck – that are suitable for small farmers. These animals are attractive and each is distinctive. Their genes are available for breeding new birds but the existing ones adapt well to their environment.

The bare neck of the Naked Neck is caused by a dominant gene and is passed to all crossbreeds. Naked Necks have 40 percent fewer feathers and are therefore better adapted to hot climates. They also have a lower protein requirement to produce feathers so the protein they consume from scratching around in the earth can be used more efficiently. This means that these birds can tolerate harsh conditions and are suitable for projects where there are insufficient financial resources to feed the hens. The same applies to the speckled black and white Venda. Not only is it a good layer, it also has a gene which makes it a good brood hen. Modern breeds are more reluctant to brood. In contrast, the Venda reproduces quickly, which means more birds are available for eating. The black Ovambo from Namibia is also suitable for harsh conditions. These hens sleep in trees at night and weigh slightly less than the other breeds but are particularly suited for the production of food protein in the poorest areas of Africa. The speckled black and white Potchefstroom Koekoek was bred in the 1940s in South Africa. As well as being a good egg producer, it provides very tasty meat. Noel Honeyborne is particularly fond of indigenous lines and for years has been searching for the best ways of preserving their genetic heritage. "Conserving the genes of animals in living populations is very expensive. It is a much better

Consorzio Ricerca Filiera Lattiero-Casearia

SICILIA

Presidenza della Regione Siciliana · Assessorato Agricoltura e Foreste · Assessorato Cooperazione, Commercio Artigianato e Pesca · Comune di Ragusa

presents

# Ragusa  Castello di Donnafugata

# Cheese ART 2002

*the renaissance of taste*

4th-9th June 2002

## EVENTS

Special guest: The American Cheese Society
Slow Food
Laboratory of taste
Food and movies
Cheesemaking in Agrigento
Cheeselandia
The market of traditional foods
Laboratory of Chef
"Cheese and Wine" the beautiful couples in the world

## SCIENTIFIC CONFERENCES

Sustainable farms system and cheeses biodiversity in Mediterranean country.

Traditional cheese production system and safety, quality and health properties of raw milk cheeses.

Potential Anti-cancer properties of cheese and dairy products.

ww.corfilac.it - cheeseart2002@tiscalinet

DDB

THE FUTURE OF WINE IN THE SIGN OF VINITALY.

www.veronafiere.it   viale del lavoro 8 37100 Verona (Italy) Tel. +39 045 829 8111

VINITALY
World Wide Wines

36TH INTERNATIONAL WINE & SPIRITS EXHIBITION.

VERONA 11-15 APRIL 2002

VERONAFIERE
I T A L Y

www.vinitaly.com

 EVENTS

 INTERNATIONAL
WINE AND SPIRIT
COMPETITION

 INTERNATIONAL
PACKAGING
COMPETITION

 enolitech
EXHIBITION OF TECHNOLOGIES
FOR VITICULTURE AND
OENOLOGY AND TECHNIQUES
FOR OLIVE GROWING AND
OLIVE OIL PRODUCTION

 SOL
INTERNATIONAL
EXHIBITION OF VIRGIN AND
EXTRA-VIRGIN OLIVE OIL

proposition to use them as part of a development project to produce food, especially for small families. Poultry are particularly suitable in this respect and we can save on the costs of maintaining genes in live populations".

The institute also carries out research on free-range farming and semi-intensive methods, comparing native and modern breeds. As Noel Honeyborne explains, "Chickens today are created for intensive farming. They would not thrive in a free-range situation. Many people today would like to have free-range farming but it must also be economically viable. There is a link between egg production and feed consumption, since free-range hens obviously require much more energy. From this point of view, indigenous breeds have an advantage".

**Fowls for Africa**

Protecting these breeds by hi-tech freezing of their genetic material would be too time-consuming and expensive. The Fowls for Africa project (FFA) is based on the idea of 'conservation through utilization', combining the production of poultry birds with know-how and research. Originally, the idea was to give support to development projects involving small farmers and poor communities but these breeds are now available elsewhere. They are used in ecotourism, in education-

al and research institutions, and on farms run by sympathetic producers. Projects outside South Africa have also made enquiries. Interest has also been shown by co-operatives that practice 'rotation farming', a combination of breeding and and arable farming. These organizations use movable cages for the chickens and move them frequently. Where the chickens leave their manure and the soil is well fertilized, vegetables are planted. In this way it is possible to produce both vegetables and animal protein within a single cycle.

Poultry production is a very important source of animal protein in rural areas of southern Africa. With the help of regional Poultry Supply Centers (PSC) the FFA is keen to support farmers. The primary aim is to produce protein simply and at low cost through the utilization of suitable breeds and appropriate technology. In addition it is intended to create jobs, to generally enhance living standards and improve the education and training of women chicken farmers. Obviously, the program is organic since the animals are free-range.

Anyone who is interested in taking part in the FFA program can do a training course obtain credit from recognized financial institutions. Poultry and special equipment can be obtained from the PSC.

The FFA network supplies the software, the necessary background information, training and veterinary care, and also the hardware, that is the poultry and additional materials such as, for example, a chicken coop for family use. It looks like a cross between a garden shed and a tent, and can be moved about and folded up easily.

Poultry Supply Centers only exist in Irene and at Glen Agricultural College in Free State Province. Noel Honeyborne is sure that this type of center has attractive business potential but there is not much interest so far. He hopes that the centers will have improved prospects when farmers are better informed about niche production of indigenous poultry breeds for healthier and more natural food.

**Chickens and Aids orphans**

Noel Honeyborne's commitment goes further. He has donated about 20 Ovambo hens to the Funanani Aids Orphans project. A group of women set up the first center for Aids orphans at Bushbuckridge, in north-east South Africa, in the mid 1990s. More than 80 orphans are now being looked after in various places. All of the women are volunteers and the centers are funded by donations.

"Women", says Honeyborne, "wondered how they could provide a better basis for the center and decided to produce eggs, first to feed the children and also earn some money. We offered them a one-week course on poultry keeping, showing them how to use the mobile cages".

In the meantime, the women of Bushbuckridge have managed to set up a small egg production unit. They use part of the earnings from the sale of eggs to purchase chicken feed, since the chickens need additional feed to produce more. Some of the eggs are given to the children to provide them with the crucial animal protein they need. The hens can be sold later on and new ones bought, or they can be eaten. Unfortunately, there are always people who take advantage of emergency situations and the Funanani Aids Orphans project has

to deal with unprincipled feed merchants who demand double the price for feed. Noel Honeyborne is looking for answers. Similar projects in Swaziland and Namibia are waiting to be supplied with hens from ARC in Irene.

With the passage of time, Noel Honeyborne's original aim to save native poultry breeds has developed into a humanitarian commitment. In so doing, he has been able to kill two birds with one stone: his chickens are multiplying, finding refuge with small farmers and at the same time providing the population with a source of food.

*Annette Frei Berthould*

---

**Motives for Slow Food Award**

Honeyborne's inspired concept with its simple slogan of 'conservation through utilization' is impressively far-sighted, displaying a profound understanding of the links between ensuring basic food supply, conserving traditional breeds that are particularly suited to local conditions, creating jobs, improving the condition of women and using environment-friendly production. Last, but not least, the project offers the prospect of creating a niche gourmet food market for its deliciously full-flavored meat. This combination of benefits for local people, ecological production and gustatory pleasure mirrors the Slow Food philosophy perfectly.

# Carlos Jorge Lewis

**Carlos Jorge Lewis, 41, has Welsh forebears and a family comprising his wife, Valentina, and their six children aged from two to 14. They live at Coronel Moldes, a town of 3,500 inhabitants, an hour's drive from Salta. This is a land of gauchos and poor farmers, of free roaming cattle, sugar cane and tobacco. It is in northwest Argentina, the Andean soul of this huge country, which is not only a mixture of tango and European melancholy but over the centuries has also held on to that part of native blood which, says Lewis, "contains genetic information on how things ought to be".**

### America, Argentina, Coronel Moldes, Province of Salta

**Tobacco, my first love**

An uncle inspired in Carlos a passion for tobacco while taking him along as a child on trips to deliver the crop to warehouses. In 1985, Carlos Lewis was awarded a degree in agriculture but even before graduating, he was working at the Mutual de Productores Tabacaleros, the tobacco growers' cooperative, and as a journalist writing on agricultural issues. He was then appointed director of the agrotechnical department at the tobacco growers' coop-

erative in Salta, completing in 1988 in a training program that took him to Zimbabwe and Cuba. In 1989, he started his own growing venture.

Tobacco now brings in a large part of his income but it is still mainly a passion, albeit an awkward one that he defends with contentious claims, such as "tobacco is healthy". He is not being provocative. It is just his drop of Indian blood talking. Curanderos, or medicine men, in the countryside still use this magic plant, the only one which does not burn or go out but smokes, to make a diagnosis or treat a patient. For the Indios, tobacco was and still is a ritual. It was smoked with other people, in meetings, when there was an important occasion and, significantly, when there was time to smoke it. They smoked less and better. Long pipes removed the source of heat from the mouth, the smoke was already cold when it arrived, and was consequently less harmful. "We need to reassess the habit. People have smoked all over the world for 5,000 years. The cigarette is the problem today but cigarettes are to tobacco what McDonald's hamburgers are to meat". What Lewis is attempting to do with the tourists who stay at his Finca Santa Anita is make them aware of the close relationship that once existed with the cultivation of tobacco. "This is knowledge which has been lost. Once, people would grow a little tobacco in their vegetable plot, to have something that gave them pleasure and they were used to smoking. It is still like that in Bolivia but nearly everywhere else in the world, including Argentina, the mystique of tobacco has been lost". Between 1988 and 1992, Lewis began to see clearly that single cultures were not the best option. That was why 1990 he started growing other crops instead of tobacco at his finca in Coronel Moldes, Santa Anita.

They were not easy times for Argentina. "They were talking about a recovery of consumption, in a country that could no longer even produce," recalls Lewis. "It looked like madness to me. The only practical solution was to live off our own resources". After years of writing articles, reflection and cautious experiments, Lewis diversified. He presented a project to the Ministry of Tourism and applied for a subsidized loan to restructure the house and turn it into a building that could accommodate tourists. To pay back the bank loan, the Lewis family gave up the house they were living in at Salta and moved to the finca. Then, with a partner in 1992, Lewis asked for another loan to start farming goats. He began with 50 or so criolla females, introducing one pardo alpino male to improve the line. With other goat farmers, he got in touch with a dairy expert and learned how to make cheese, which he began to produce and sell in 1993. He founded goat farmers' association with 14 members. It no longer exists because the farmers had to cope with the crisis and focus on safer and more conventional activities. Still, Lewis hopes to revive it soon.

Tobacco supports the economy of the whole area. Farmers take their crop to collection centers, which supply national and multinational manufacturers. The years between 1992 and 1996 were excellent and enabled Lewis to develop other projects. In 1995, he opened a bakery in town. When the cyclical downturn came in 1997, the new ventures

were under way and on August 20 1998, he opened the Finca Santa Anita farm holiday center.

## What do you do?

The Ingeniero, as they call him – the faculty of agriculture in South America is part of the Polytechnic and graduates earn the title of 'Engineer' – is a man of a thousand activities and a thousand skills. He is President of the Chamber of Tobacco in Salta, and this has helped gain him the esteem of his fellow citizens. Recently he was also appointed 'Secretario de Producción' for the province of Salta, a sort of councillor with responsibility for the economy. But that's not all. In little more than ten years, he has managed to put together a web of activities involving the whole community. Here are some pieces of the puzzle.

**Algarrobo**. The name is reminiscent of the European carob but it is a misnomer. To the Spaniards who arrived in America, looked like the European species (*Ceratonia siliqua*) but in fact it belongs to a different species (*Prosopis alba*). Andean people frequently just call it arbol, 'tree', as it is so common. Lewis began to get interested in the algarrobo in 1994 as a source of animal fodder.

The fruit of the algarrobo is a clear thin pod containing small seeds. It falls from the tree in January, as soon as it has ripened. It is therefore picked from the ground but this has to be done quickly so that it is not damaged by moisture or by animals, such as goats, donkeys, cows, birds and so on, which are very fond of it. It is a spontaneous tree that is difficult to grow. The wood is excellent for making furniture, as well as firewood, which has led to its being felled indiscriminately. Andean tradition assigns various uses to the algarrobo: its fruit used to be ground to obtain the flour for a drink, aloja. Every year shortly before the algarrobo season, Lewis places posters in his bakery, or advertises on local radio, to say that he is keen to buy algarrobas. "Someone should buy it. People then realize the tree has value". Using algarroba flour, you can make excellent traditional pastries which the Finca Santa Anita includes on its menu in season.

**Goats**. After the Pardo Alpino had been introduced, it was then the turn of another male, from the Saanen breed, whose line is today being selected. The present flock comprises 200 goats, about 70 of which produce milk. The kids are usually left with the mothers, since goat meat is also sold and the longer they are suckled, the better their meat is. In any case, there is no market for the cheese the goats could produce. Lewis periodically gives kids to others with small flocks in the area so as to introduce selected animals into other flocks.

# Complete your collection

no. 1

no. 2

no. 3

no. 4

no. 5

no. 6

no. 7

no. 8

no. 9

no. 10

no. 11

no. 12

To obtain back issues contact:
Slow Food Editore - Fax ++39 0172 411218
E-mail: slowinfo@slowfood.com

Slow Food

# Join the Slow Food Movement!

Slow Food

## WHAT IS SLOW FOOD?

It is an international movement with 60.000 members and more than 400 convivia (chapters) in 35 countries of the world, which focuses on conviviality, hospitality, education in taste and promotion of food culture.

Slow food is aimed at food and wine enthusiasts, those who do not want to lose the myriad tastes of traditional foodstuffs from around the world and those who share the snail's wise slowitude.

## WHAT IS *SLOW*?

It is the quarterly review of the movement, a platform for encounter and information, study, entertainment and pleasure. Published in Italian, English, German, Spanish and French editions, it is the official Slow Food magazine and is sent to all members.

The aim of Slow is to spread the basic principles of the movement and collect the ensuing ideas and contributions.

Its success had made it a truly international polyglot.

Slow Food - via Mendicità Istruita, 14 - 12042 Bra (Cn) Italy - Tel. ++39 0172 419611 - Fax ++39 0172 421293

**Cheese**. Cheese is made with pasteurized milk, as laid down by the law, and is sold at a shop selling specialty foodstuffs at Salta airport. However, it is mainly served – and sold – to guests at the farm holiday center. "Tourists are vital to marketing goat's cheese", observes Lewis, "because this type of cheese is exotic and rarely consumed at home on a regular basis". Goat's cheese can be a tourist attraction and gourmet highlight of the area. Following the success of Finca Santa Anita, other farm holiday centers are starting up, gradually putting the whole area in a food and drink tourism circuit.

**Chili pepper**. Another indigenous crop that Lewis has revived is chili pepper. He grows two varieties, criollo and cayena. The latter is incredibly hot. Just handling it during the harvest causes irritation to the hands and eyes. For this reason, it is getting increasingly difficult to find workers and it is even harder to find farmers who are willing to grow it. But the results of this potent spice in cooking are wonderful and Lewis does not want to see it disappear. He continues to grow chili peppers and sell them dried.

**Charqui**. This is meat, usually beef, that has been dried in freezing cold. Charqueador is another disappearing occupation. It requires patience, delicacy and knowledge of anatomy. The animal is filleted and the meat is left under salt overnight. Then comes the delicate work: the muscle is cut into very thin, long strips which are then hung for ten days in the frost and sun of a dry Andean winter. The dried meat will keep until the following year. Lewis looked for, and found, the last charqueador in Coronel Moldes. He was working at a farm doing other work because it was no longer possible to live just by making charqui. His extraordinary skill risks extinction unless apprentices can be found. Charqui is a wonderful food, used in many of the most flavorsome recipes of the traditional cuisine.

**Leather**. The hide from butchered cattle and goats is used to make saddles and other accessories for horses. Every time he is needed, the tanner arrives at the finca with his equipment. His craft is another one in decline. In his skilled hands, the leather gradually takes shape and finds yet another way of talking about this land. The saddles are then used on farm horses, sold or, most often, bartered for animals or goods.

**Horses**. All northern Argentinians have a passionate love of horses, which are often indispensable. In many bush areas, there is no other transport. Lewis keeps two breeds of horses, criollos and the so-called Peruvian paso horses. The latter are particularly sought-after and often used for parades. They move very elegantly because they walk with a four-beat gait, moving each leg separately instead of the usual movement of two legs moving diagonally together. This means that their back remains level and the rider doesn't bob up and down. Peruvian paso horses were used for getting around the plantations and supervising work. They are not suitable for long distances or awkward mountain tracks since they get tired quickly. Criollos, on the other hand, are strong, big-boned horses, good for riding in mountains and forests for the long hours that gauchos spend in the saddle. They are less highly regarded but more useful, and it is important that genetic improvements should continue to be made by selective breeding. The fashion for the admittedly fascinating Peruvian paso horses should not get out of hand.

**Farm holidays**. The farm can accommodate about 20 people in attractive spacious rooms. Tourists can take part in all the activities of the farm or go pony trekking into the nearby mountains, where some interesting archaeological sites can be found. "Agricultural tourism is a means and an end," says Lewis. "Maintaining the farm involves considerable fixed costs and money earned from tourism is immediately available. But the opposite is also true. Everything that we do has become closely connected to the interest which it can generate in visitors.

The craftsman who works leather would do it anyway but if he does it surrounded by a group of people who look on admiringly and ask a thousand questions, he ends up doing it with more enthusiasm. He has company; he works more contentedly. And his son may realize that he can meet the world while carrying on his father's occupation and staying in Coronel Moldes".

**Regional cuisine**. The cooking comes from Valentina's side of the family. "The women in my wife's family", says Lewis admiringly, "have a talent for cooking, and an enthusiasm and scholarly respect for recipes, while being able to adapt them to circumstances. In particular, they have a feeling for things that are well prepared, wholesome and attractive to look at". The women are also good to watch as they work together. Valentina, is assisted by Santos, the only full-time employee, and on important occasions also by her mother and Paula, her eldest daughter. Dishes rich in history and flavor take form, starting from carefully measured ingredients: the results are an elegant compromise between respect for tradition and modern demands.

*Cinzia Scaffidi*

---

### Motives for Slow Food Award

It is a small, peaceful, daily battle. A battle of intelligence and farsightedness against fear and blinkered attitudes in a country where the economic crisis has dragged on for at least 15 years, undermining people's strength and assets. The activities at Finca Santa Anita are bringing economic benefits, development and work. As well as confidence, roots and identity. Old crops are being grown again; old occupations are returning; love of the land and natural resources is being restored. And if foreign tourists are fascinated by the beauty and passion that permeate all the activities at the finca, Argentine visitors can think of their stay as a short training course in economics and sustainable development. The Slow Food Award is also an acknowledgement of the perseverance and the serenity with which this alternative route has been followed, and the community spirit which has inspired it from the beginning.

# Necton Companhia Portuguesa de Culturas Marinhas

**J**oao Navalho was born in Mozambique in 1965 of Portuguese parents and moved to Lisbon as a child. He earned his degree in marine biology and a graduate degree in aquaculture at Algarve University. He and Victor Verdello, a friend at the Biotechnology Institute of the Catholic University in Oporto, applied for and received a grant to look for innovative ways to use Portugal's natural resources. Portugal needed to take advantage of the Algarve's sun and sea in ways that went beyond the bargain-basement tourism catering for planeloads of German and English visitors.

The two students thought they could use new technology to make large quantities of algae that produce beta carotene, which is valuable to food producers seeking a healthful, non-chemical alternative orange dye. In 1994, they began looking for a part of Portugal with maximum sunlight and plentiful clean seawater to optimize algae production. After several years of searching, they found the perfect spot: 12

hectares of salt marshes in the protected National Park of Ria Formosa, in the tidal flats just a few kilometers from the tourist resorts of Olhao and Faro. Seville is just 150 kilometers away, Lisbon 300. The constant flow of seawater, free of polluting effluents from the industries that mar much of the Atlantic coastline, and the relentless sunshine would be ideal for the cutting-edge technology they planned to install.

In 1997, the pair formed a company called Necton. A few grants and their own skills would be their capital, and they would run the company on socialist ideals. All workers, whatever their position, would be the majority stockholders and share profits. Then something got in the way of their progressive plans, something no idealistic marine biologist could ignore. That something was the ancient history of their carefully selected site as one of the world's primary producers of a product man can't live without - salt.

## Europe, Portugal, Ria Formosa National Park, Algarve

### Flamingo-covered wetlands

The Egyptians were probably the first to systematically evaporate seawater to extract salt and the Phoenicians probably brought this rudimentary technology to the Portuguese Atlantic coast. The presence of Roman ruins in the Algarve suggests that salt was produced there, as it was on much of the coastline. What is certain is that by the year 1000, the Algarve was sending

*Joao Navalho*

salt to the rest of Europe, and in the 15th and 16th centuries, the Age of Exploration, salt helped Portugal consolidate her position as a world power. But the countries of northern and eastern Europe learned to mine rock salt in caves and in the mid 20th century, mechanization in the mines, cheap transport and better roads across the Continent made sea salt relatively expensive. Mechanization also arrived for the sea salt, including production in the Algarve. After the Second World War, the marenotos, the salt pan workers, found they couldn't compete with cheaper rock salt, and abandoned their work to find jobs in factories and cities. Portuguese sea salt, even if mechanically harvested, maintained its high reputation. Large conglomerates sell Portuguese sea salt to the French, for table use, and ship inferior salt back to Portugal. But the small salt pans that had kept local economies and agricultural artisans alive vanished.

It upset Navalho and his co-workers to see small salt pans on their own and adjoining property abandoned to become communal dumping grounds. Private land ownership is allowed within the large national park, as long as it is for nonpolluting agricultural use. But the only businesses they saw around them were mechanized fish farms and huge salt pans that computers could regulate with almost no help from workmen and that machines could harvest once a year. The rest, the network of small rectangular salt pans that followed the sluices of the intertidal shores, where sea water to fill the pans was most easily available, had been almost completely abandoned. The ecosystem the network supported was vanishing too. "The place was like a desert," Navalho, a study in perpetual motion, informs visitors to Necton. "If you don't fill the pans with water every year and you're not taking care of them every day, they'll be dirty, dry and ugly. And the birds move on, not just flamingos but all the others, avocets, plovers and egrets".

The new collaborators faced an urgent, major change of plan. Their first commitment was to the environment, and that meant keeping the wetlands wet. One marenoto, Maximino Guerreiro, was already looking after the industrial-size salt pan on Necton's property. He warned the new owners that they would have to take care of the smaller pans, too, if they didn't want to watch them turn into dumps like the ones they saw on their morning rides to work. Besides, he said, the smaller salinas were harvested several times over the summer rather than once at the end, ahead of the fall rains. Their salt tasted better and was much healthier, too. But Necton had to act quickly. Men like him were a dying breed. Maximino had been born to a knowledge of how to fill the pans in the spring and, when enough water had evaporated and crystals had formed to harvest the salt with wooden rakes. But he could show them how it was done.

To take Guerreiro up on his offer, Necton found another collaborator, Yago Del Valle Inclan, an industrial engineer who had also worked in aquaculture on the southern Spanish coastline. Valle Inclan, in Galicia and raised in Barcelona, preferred country life to the rush of the city was ready to apply his modern knowledge to old techniques. Valle Inclan arrived in the late fall of 1997, the time when salt harvesters take a long break before preparing the salt pans for the next spring. He spent long hours and days with Guerreiro, learning about water levels from month to month during the salt season, how to gauge evaporation, how to look at salt crystals and know when to rake the salt. He told Guerreiro about algae, explained the food chain and saltwater wetland ecology.

The men found and repaired the tools, then cleaned out the clay-bottomed salt pans. They cleared the channels of water

that would use gravity and the tides to replenish the salt pans. Through the spring and summer of 1998, they tended the pans, with the help of a few young workers Guerreiro trained during the busy times, the salt harvest, which happens every five to seven weeks. At the end of the summer, Necton had a crop of dazzlingly white salt. The young executives were thrilled. They had a marvelous product. Then they tried to sell it, and quickly realized why they saw so much trash instead of salt on their way to and from work.

**"Regards, c'est blanc!"**

According to Portuguese law, Necton cannot sell table salt. In 1973, the government set new standards defining three categories of salt. The highest was pure sodium chloride, which is what industry wants as a primary ingredient in glass, paints, batteries, explosives, glues and plastics. This is also the salt most people buy for the table. Additives such as iodine and fluoride are allowed for table salt, as well as potassium cyanide and aluminum silicate as anti-caking agents, to prevent the refined salt from turning to stone. The second category is 96 percent sodium chloride, and the third is less than 96 percent sodium chloride, for use on the roads, not at table (the main use

of salt around the world is as a de-icing agent). Necton's salt fell into this third category. Hand-harvested, sun-dried sea salt has a far greater variety of mineral salts than plain, purified sodium chloride. Some, like magnesium, iron, and calcium, are present in relatively large quantities. It also contains many micronutrients that get washed out of mechanical salt along with all the other impurities that machines introduce. This makes traditional sea salt far better for the consumer's health, as well as giving it much flavor. But as far as the Portuguese authorities were concerned, all unwashed, unpurified sea salt is unfit for human consumption. The best Necton could do that first year was to sell its salt at the same price the mechanically harvested crop from the one large salt pan would fetch, despite the fact that hand-harvested salt requires ten times as much labor. Frustrated, the young partners sent Valle Inclan to visit the cooperative at Guerande, in France on the Atlantic coast. Since its foundation in 1975, its fleur de sel gas become a legend in the gourmet world. Fleur de sel is the cream of the salt harvest, the newly formed crystals that float on the surface before becoming big and heavy enough to fall to the bottom. They must be harvested quickly, within hours of forming, before they precipitate. Although the content and health benefits of fleur de sel and traditional sea salt are identical, what's different is the texture: fleur de sel crumbles at a touch and melts on the tongue. Valle Inclan learned a great deal about methods for harvesting from his French hosts, and came back convinced that the Necton partners were sitting on a gold mine. His conviction was based on what inspired the exclamation of the head of Guerande when he first saw a basket of fleur de sel at Necton, "Regards, c'est blanc!" Portugal has many advantages over the Brittany coast where the French harvest their own premium salt. Rain stirs up the salt crystals in the salt pan, which as they become more numerous precipitate to the clay bottom of the shallow pan. The sun that brought the young marine biologists to the Algarve is far more reliable than on the north coast of France, where workers must harvest salt even after rainfalls. The elegant-sounding sel gris of Brittany gets its gray color from the clay that is raked along with the salt crystals: mud, to put it bluntly. Necton decided from the first to leave the bottom layer of the pans untouched by the workers' wooden rakes, resulting in a white so pure that the tall pyramid-shaped piles of salt from each harvest look like

miniature Alps or Pyrenees in the blinding light of a winter's day. It's a disorienting image in the relentless heat of the Algarve summer. French fleur de sel was whiter than sel gris, or traditional sea salt. But Necton's flor de sal was even whiter. And still illegal.

Necton found a way around its problems with the help of the Reserva Natural de Castro Marim, a reserve in the Algarve where another producer was still producing traditional sea salt. A technician at the reserve named Anabela Resende had brought together a few marenotos who wanted to harvest sea salt by hand to form a producer's association, TradiSal. Necton joined in 1999, bringing the total to ten members. Resende knew of a certification that the leading French organic-food group, Nature et Progrès, granted to unrefined sea salt. It guarantees that the salt has been tested for, and found free of, 82 possible contaminants. The group requires producers to work in protected areas where industry and hunting are forbidden, and that they sun-dry and do not grind their salt. Winning this certification has the extra benefit for Necton of demonstrating that the algae it plans to sell is produced in a pure environment.

But it won't change the antiquated Portuguese law. TradiSal is petitioning the government to exclude two categories from the restrictions of the infamous third class: traditional sea salt and flor de sal. It also wants to create an internationally recognized logo that will appear on each bag of these two kinds of salt, to create a market that will appreciate the difference, and pay accordingly.

*Corby Kummer*

---

**Motives for Slow Food Award**

The cultural heritage relating to the conservation of small salinas, a whole language of terms for tools, the cycle of tending and cleaning and harvesting, is being lost with the marenotos. With the salt pans goes a fragile ecosystem, a rare instance of the survival in a highly populated area. It is the world's most productive ecosystem after rain forests.

The founders of the young company can't afford to go on selling their salt at a loss. Already Necton sells its traditional sea salt in bulk to France, where demand far outweighs its supply. Pure white traditional Portuguese salt is much more delicate, and closer to fleur de sel, than virtually any sea salt now on the market. But it is almost unknown outside Portugal, and what little is available is likely to have a French label. In addition, virtually none of the connoisseurs of fleur de sel, who are the only consumers prepared to pay a premium for salt, knows that an excellent and, many would say, superior version is being sold in Portugal at a fraction of the price.

Necton wants to preserve an endangered tradition, and the endangered environment that goes along with it, before turning to its original project: algae. TradiSal is still exploring ways to cooperate without being a full-fledged cooperative. There are no funds to pool together, particularly for the publicity and marketing that are essential to launch flor de sal. Navalho wants to avoid marketing colored aromaitized salts, as other traditional producers have done. He dreams of being able to persuade young people to continue an ancient tradition, and earn enough to make them want to hand it down to their own children.

Special Jury Award

# Predrag Peca Petrovic

**P**redrag Peca Petrovic was born on 25 May 1949 in Pastric, a small village close to the town of Mionica, in northwest Serbia, about 80 kilometers south of Belgrade. He grew up in a farming family in poor farming and woodland country, respecting nature and forming a strong bond with the land of his birth. A model student during his school career, he had to move to Belgrade to attend high school, where he later graduated in biology with top marks. His time at university was a key moment in his life, since the lure of academe was tempting him away from the countryside, to which Petrovic continued to feel drawn. His professors recognized his brilliant talents and suggested he became a research assistant. So Petrovic spent the late 1970s attempting to combine his passions for science and nature, helped by his involvement in the expeditions which the Belgrade Institute for Medical Research organized to various parts of the world. The young Petrovic's main interest was bats, particularly vampire bats, which he studied in Costa Rica, Nicaragua and Colombia as a guest of the Institute for Tropical Research in Panama.

When he returned to his region, he was at last able to devote himself to his abiding passion and become involved in the protection of biodi-

versity in all its manifestations. During the 1980s, he was a people's representative and professor but would still work on the farm whenever he went home. When lecturing in the schools of Mionica, he always encouraged the young people of the area not to abandon their fathers' customs and trades, to protect wildlife and plants and proudly dedicate themselves to safeguarding ecosystems in the surrounding district of Valjevo.

Petrovic has now permanently given up his teaching career and spends his time discovering and breeding native species and growing rare fruit. His work hinges around a project which is the pride of the Yugoslav environmental scene, the Mionica Association of Ecological Research. Thanks to Petrovic's work, the local authorities have declared the whole area around Pastric a 'protected nature park'. After years of being shunned by the regime, he has been appointed by the present government as a consultant and advisor to revive agriculture in this enchanting corner of Serbia, with its wooded hills that open out into magnificent high pastures.

Petrovic continues to live in Pastric, in a stone house full of animals and surrounded by orchards, where he is a full-time farmer. His love for nature and his mission to protect biodiversity are shared by his elderly but sprightly parents Stenoje and Rada, his charming wife Dana and their two daughters, Jelena, 18, and Ivana, 10.

# Europe, Serbia, Mionica

## From vampires to pigs

Vampire bats may sound exotic, a note to enhance Petrovic's air of magic and mystery. The fact is that just a short distance from his farm is a fantastic cave which, thanks to underground air currents, has a range of different microclimates and is home to 15 or so species of bat, eight of which extremely rare elsewhere in Europe. Peca Petrovic has spent 118 nights in the cave, studying and ringing the bats to find out about their migrations, habits and behavior. Now that people know about the bats in the cave, Petrovic and some friends are going to build a sundial above the entrance, with a sign warning about the adders he intends to introduce into the area. "I'm doing this to protect both the tourists and the bats," he explains. "We have to discourage tourists from entering, since the bats need peace and quiet".

The adders are an almost superfluous precaution, however, as opposite the cavern flows a river that serves as an additional deterrent to unwary visitors.

This river, the Ribnica, is the scene of other initiatives which reveal Petrovic's love for the treasures of his land. About 500 otters, also endangered, live in this stretch of water and the biologist reckons they are vital for the health of the river. Because of his prestigious academic background, not to mention the eccentricity of abandoning a university career to return to the land, local farmers and young people regard him as a kind of guru. So does the national government. If Petrovic promises that a law will soon be passed to ban otter hunting and that a section of the river will be fenced off, he knows what he's talking about.

Petrovic is also proposing a similar measure to safeguard snails. He wants to discourage people from collecting them in the woods and encourage their breeding. In his campaign to protect the traditional frog and salamander-filled farm ponds, Petrovic brought in well-known scientists to persuade the farmers not to fill them in. The farmers felt flattered to have the ear of important people from the city. They had never imagined they could possibly be important enough to provoke such interest and, it goes without saying, they listened to Petrovic's advice in this case too.

But the most important initiative in the whole area is the Mionica Association of Ecological Research, which buys flocks and herds of native breeds, obtained wherever they can be found or bred over the years, and then entrusts individual animals to the area's farmers, according to demand and the availability of time and feed. The farmers can keep the milk, cheese and young animals, undertaking to give the animals back after three or four years. The population of native breeds thus increases while local people are rescued from poverty and emigration. Petrovic knows the farmers personally and decides who will get the animals. 'Foster farmers' are invited not to despoil the landscape and to rear the animals using traditional methods. A collective awareness of tradition and local character has been spread, along with a belief in organic farming, which affects the area in every way imaginable. Recipes of the past are being revived and efforts are being made to protect and promote traditional farming techniques. Not least, rural architecture, which has so far been preserved almost intact, is being protected.

Many breeds are involved in the project. There are three types of cow, the busa, so hardy and adaptable it is called the 'mother of the poor', the podolska and the kolubarska, a graceful animal with impressive horns, farmed for meat and milk). Five breeds of sheep, sjenicka, krivo-virska, lipska, vitoroga pivska and pramenka, are involved as are three attractive breeds of pig, the mangulica, the black resavka and the moravka, whose skin is covered with a strange, goat-like wool and which farmers in Belgium and Hungary are attempting to breed. The work with pigs is particularly commendable at a time when Europe is losing the variety and character of its sausages and salamis because of the prevalence of just two breeds, the large white and the duroc. All the breeds mentioned number only a few hundred animals at present, and only the commitment of the Mionica Association of Ecological Research to classifying and breeding is keeping them alive.

The same goes for plants. True to his credo that you cannot do science and research without practical work in the field, Petrovic has turned to growing, and then giving away to farmers, who actually pay a token fee of two marks, ancient native varieties: vines, medicinal plants, valieski raspberries a very full-flavored variety, once the area's main export crop, apples, pears, cherries and plums. These last are the source of three sugar-free jams, vinegar and the legendary rakija, the plum brandy that Serbs always offer you at the start of a meal, breakfast included. "*Homo sapiens* is an evolutionary dead-end. We have to turn back

to improve," maintains Petrovic. "I am waiting for a new development that will stop this senseless progress. And when it comes, I will be ready to become its high priest. Today, I feel the support of the country and it is good to see that the isolation I once suffered, when I was seen as the only intellectual who had failed to make his mark in the city, has now been transformed into requests for advice and unconditional support. Even the government comes to ask for my advice".

## The Village of Misic

In Petrovic's future plans is an ambitious project called 'The Village of Misic', which will be inaugurated next year. It will be set up at Struganik and is named after duke Zivojin Misic, a Yugoslav national hero from the First World War. He taught strategy at the Military Academy in peacetime from 1898 to 1904 and is remembered for his victories over the Austro-Hungarian army in Kosovo in 1915 and for the battle of Salonica the following year. The general's house is still standing in Struganik, as is a Serbian Orthodox church dedicated to St Peter and St Paul and a 19th century school, which will become the home of the far-sighted biodiversity project. It will host scientists and visitors, who will be able to study or see for the first time the ancient native breeds which Petrovic has been rescuing, protecting, breeding and giving to local farmers over the last decade or so.

The Village of Misic will have herds and flocks of native breeds, a snail farm, fields for growing medicinal plants and orchards of native Serb varieties. It will be an environmental landmark, which scientists will visit to carry out research while ordinary people will come to observe the production of specialty foods firsthand. It will be possible to see how cheese is made and how animals are bred, to eat local produce and to spend the night in the nature park. In addition, many young people from Mionica will have the opportunity learn traditional techniques and then work locally in the village or in the fields. In this way, they will not be forced to migrate to factories in the city.

*Alessandro Monchiero*

### Motives for Slow Food Award

Petrovic has twice been 'distracted' from his work by war, serving as a soldier in Herzegovina and in Kosovo. The year 1999 was Petrovic's personal and professional annus horribilis. After the war ended, the inhabitants of the Valjevo region not only had to endure the hardships imposed by sanctions, they also suffered an earthquake of 5.7 on the Richter scale, one of the five most serious earthquakes in Serbia in the last 100 years. The epicenter was located in Mionica itself and neighboring towns. The disaster caused considerable damage to the buildings being renovated to create the Village of Misic at Struganik.

Peca Petrovic deserves the Slow Food Award for what he has accomplished in the past and for what he is doing now. He has rekindled environmental awareness in a war-torn, poverty-stricken region oppressed by a dictatorship, and made it a role model for the other regions in the Serb Republic. But his project for the future also merits an award for it will require substantial funding to be completed. Petrovic is fully aware that he cannot expect everything to happen immediately but the protection of the region's genetic heritage was his first priority. This part of the work is progressing rapidly and a great deal has been done over the last ten years. To complete the Village of Misic, Petrovic has to hope for help from well-wishers, the Yugoslav government and the Slow Food Award.

# The custodians

*Vandana Shiva*

**W**omen are the leading experts in, and custodians of, biodiversity. They have been society's seed keepers, food processors and healers. And biodiversity itself has been venerated in female form. The indigenous communities of the Andes see corn, potato, coca and quinoa as goddesses. The ancient Rig Veda hymn worships healing plants as mothers.

*Mothers, you have a hundred forms*
*and a thousand revelations.*
*You who have a hundred ways of working,*
*make this man whole for me.*
*Be joyful, you plants that bear flowers*
*and you that bear fruit.*
*Like mares that win the race together,*
*the growing plants will carry us to the other side.*
*You mothers called plants, I say*
*to you who are goddesses,*
*let me win a horse, a cow, a robe*
*– and your very life, O man.*
*When I take these plants in my hand,*
*yearning for the victory prize,*
*the life of the disease vanishes as if before*
*a hunter holding onto life itself.*
*From him through whom you plants creep*
*limb by limb, joint by joint,*
*you banish disease like a giant coming between fighters.*
*Fly away, disease, along with the*
*blue jay and the jay;*
*disappear with the howling of the wind,*
*and with the rain storm.*
*Let one help the other;*
*let one stand by the other.*
*All of you working together, hear*
*this prayer of the soul.*

*Photo Granata*

The rise of industrial medicine and industrial agriculture was based on a war against biodiversity and women. The witch hunts of Europe were an attack on women as experts.

The myth that the scientific revolution was a universal process of intellectual progress is constantly undermined by feminist studies and the history of the science of non-western cultures. These link the rise of reductionism to the subordination and destruction of women's knowledge in the west, and the knowledge of non-western cultures. The witch-hunts of Europe were largely a process of undermining the authority, and destroying the expertise, of European women. In 1511, the English Parliament passed an act directed against 'common artificers, as smythes, weavers and women who attempt great cures and things of great difficulties: in the witch they partly use sorcerye and witch-craft'. By the 16th century, women in Europe were totally excluded from the practice of medicine and healing because 'wise women' ran the risk of being declared witches. A deeper, more violent form of exclusion of women's knowledge and expertise, and of the knowledge of tribal and peasant cultures, is now under way with the spread of the male-centered paradigm of science. This marginalizes women and destroys biodiversity. It is pushing millions of people to starvation and millions of species to extinction.

## Who feeds the world?

My answer is very different to that given by most people. It is women and small farmers working with biodiversity who are the primary food providers in the Third World. Contrary to the popular assumption, their biodiversity-based small farm systems are more productive than industrial single crop systems.

Diversity and sustainable systems of food production have been destroyed in the name of increasing food production. However, the destruction of diversity is accompanied by the disappearance of important sources of nutrition. When measured in terms of nutrition per acre, and biodiversity, the so called 'high yields' of industrial agriculture do not imply more production of food and better nutrition. 'Yield' usually refers to production per unit area of a single crop. 'Production' refers to the total harvest of several different crops. Planting only one crop in the entire field as a monoculture will of course increase its yield. Planting multiple crops in a mixture will entail low yields of individual crops but a high total production of food. Yields have been defined in such a way as to eclipse food

*Tibet. Photo Brian A Uikander, Corbis/Grazia Neri*

production on small farms by small farmers. This obscures the production by millions of women farmers in the Third World, farmers like those in the my native Himalayas who fought against logging in the Chipko movement, who in their terraced fields grow amaranth and various kinds of soybean, millet, beans and peas. From the point of view of biodiversity, biodiversity-based productivity is superior to single-crop productivity. I call this blindness to the high productivity of diversity a 'monoculture of the mind', which creates single crops in our fields.

The Mayan peasants in Chiapas are called unproductive because they produce only two tons of corn per acre. However, the overall food output is 20 tons per acre when the variety of beans, squashes, vegetables and fruit trees is taken into account. In Java, small farmers cultivate 607 species in their home gardens, with an overall species diversity comparable to a deciduous tropical forest. In sub-Saharan Africa, women cultivate as many as 120 different plants in the spaces left among the cash crops. A single home garden in Thailand has more than 230 species, and African home gardens have more than 60 species of trees. Rural families in the Congo eat leaves from more than 50 different species of trees. A study in eastern Nigeria found that home gardens occupying only two per cent of a household's farmland accounted for half of the farm's total output. Similarly, home gardens in Indonesia are estimated to provide more than 20 per cent of household income and 40 per cent of domestic food supplies.

Research done by the UN's Food and Agriculture Organization has shown that small biodiverse farms can produce thousands of times more food than large, industrial monocultures. Diversity is the best strategy for preventing drought and desertification. What the world needs to feed a growing population sustainably is more intense biodiversity, not the increasing use of chemicals or genetic engineering. Although women and small peasants feed the world through biodiversity, we are repeatedly told that without genetic engineering and the globalization of agriculture the world will starve. In spite of all empirical evidence showing that genetic engineering does not produce more food and in fact often leads to a net decline in yields, it is constantly promoted as the only option to feed the hungry.

This deliberate blindness to diversity, the blindness to nature's production, production by women, and production by Third World farmers, allows destruction and appropriation to be projected as creation. Take the case of the much derided 'golden rice', or geneti-

*Saint-Vincent, Antille, Israele. Photos Ted Spiegel and Paul A Souders, Corbis/Grazia Neri*

cally engineered vitamin A rice as a cure for blindness. It is assumed that without genetic engineering, we cannot eliminate vitamin A deficiency. However, nature gives us many plentiful sources of vitamin A. If rice was not polished, rice itself would provide vitamin A. If herbicides were not sprayed on our wheat fields, we would have bathua, amaranth, mustard leaves as a delicious and nutritious greens. Women in Bengal use more than 150 plants as greens. Here are a few: hinche sak (*Enhydra fluctuans*), palang sak (*Spinacea oleracea*), tak palang (*Rumex vesicarius*), lal sak (*Amaranthus gangeticus*), champa note (*Amaranthus tristis*), gobra note (*Amaranthus lividus*), ghenti note (*Amaranthus tennifolius*), banspata note (*Amaranthus lanceolatus*), ban note (*Amaranthus viridis*), sada note (*Amaranthus blitum*), kanta note (*Amaranthus spinosus*), bethua sale (*Chenopodium album*), brahmi sak (*Bacopa monrieri*) and sushin sak (*Marulea quadrifolio*), to name but a few. But the myth of creation presents biotechnologists as the creators of vitamin A, denying nature's many gifts and women's knowledge of how to use this diversity to feed their children and families.

## Capitalist patriarchs

The most efficient means of bringing about the destruction of nature, local economies and small autonomous producers is to render their production invisible. Women are considered by their families and communities to be 'nonproductive' and 'economically inactive'. The devaluation of women's work, and of work done in sustainable economies, is the natural outcome of a system constructed by a capitalist patriarchy. This is how globalization destroys local economies; the destruction itself is counted as growth. Women themselves are devalued. Because much of their work in rural and indigenous communities is undertaken in collaboration with nature, and is often in conflict with the dominant market-driven development and trade policies, and because work that satisfies needs and ensures sustenance is devalued in general, there is less attention given to life and life support systems. The devaluation and invisibility of sustainable, regenerative production is most glaring in the area of food. While a patriarchal division of labor has assigned women the role of feeding their families and communities, patriarchal economies and patriarchal views of science and technology magically make women's work in providing food disappear. 'Feeding the world' becomes disassociated from the women who actually do it and is projected as dependent on global agribusiness and biotechnology corporations. Howev-

er, industrialization, the genetic engineering of food and the globalization of trade in agriculture are recipes for creating hunger, not for
feeding the poor.

Everywhere, food production is becoming a loss-creating economy,
with farmers spending more buying costly inputs for industrial production than the price they receive for their produce. The consequence is rising debts and suicides in both rich and poor countries.
Economic globalization is leading to concentration in the seed industry, the increased use of pesticides and, finally, increased debt.
Capital-intensive, corporate-controlled agriculture is spreading into
regions where peasants are poor but had been, until now, self-suffi-
cient in food. In the regions where industrial agriculture has been
introduced through globalization, higher costs are making it virtually impossible for small farmers to survive. The globalization of non-
sustainable industrial agriculture is decimating the incomes of Third
World farmers with a combination of currency devaluation, increases in production costs and the collapse of commodity prices.

Farmers everywhere are being paid a fraction of what they received
for the same commodity a decade ago. In the USA, wheat prices at
the farm dropped from USD 5.75 a bushel to USD 2.43; soybean
prices dropped from USD 8.40 to USD 4.29; and corn prices fell
from USD 4.43 to USD 1.72. In India from 1999 to 2000, prices for
coffee dropped from R 60 to R 18 per kilogram while prices of oil
seeds declined by more than 30 percent. The Canadian National
Farmers Union put it like this in a report to the senate this year.
While the farmers growing cereals – wheat, oats, corn – earn negative returns and are pushed into bankruptcy, the companies that
make breakfast cereals reap huge profits. In 1998, cereal companies
Kellogg's, Quaker Oats, and General Mills enjoyed return on equity
rates of 56, 165 and 222 percent, respectively. While a bushel of
corn sold for less than USD 4, a bushel of cornflakes cost USD 133.
In 1998, the cereal companies were 186 to 740 times more profitable than the farms. Farmers may be making too little because
others are taking too much (National Farmers Union, 2000).

A World Bank report has admitted that behind the polarization of
domestic consumer prices and world prices are large trading companies in international commodity markets. If farmers earn less, consumers, especially in poor countries, pay more. In India, food prices
doubled from 1999 to 2000 and consumption of food cereals
dropped by 12 percent in rural areas, increasing the food depriva-
tion of the already undernourished and pushing up mortality rates.

*Peru. Photo Stuard Franklin, Magnum*
*Mongolia. Photo Eve Arnold, Magnum*

Economic growth through global commerce is based on pseudosur-
pluses. More food is being traded while the poor are consuming less.
When growth increases poverty, when real production becomes a
negative economy, and speculators are called wealth creators, something has gone wrong with the concepts and categories of wealth
and wealth creation. Pushing the real production by nature and people into a negative economy implies that production of real goods
and services is declining, creating deeper poverty for the millions
who are not part of the dotcom route to instant wealth.

Women, as I have said, are the world's primary food producers and
processors. However, their work in production and processing has
now become invisible. According to the McKinsey corporation,
American food giants recognize that Indian agribusiness has lots of
room to grow, especially in food processing. India processes a mi-
nuscule one percent of the food it grows, compared with 70 percent
for the US, Brazil and the Philippines. It is not that we Indians eat
our food raw. Global consultants simply fail to see the 99 percent
food processing done by women at household level, or by small cot-
tage industries, because they are not controlled by global agribusiness. Ninety nine per cent of India's agriprocessing has been deliber-
ately kept at household level. Now, under the pressure of globalization, things are changing. Pseudohygiene laws, which shut down the
food economy based on local small scale processing under community control, are part of the arsenal of global agribusiness to establish
market monopolies by force and coercion, not competition. In August 1998, small scale local processing of edible oil was banned in
India by a packaging order, which made sale of unpackaged oil illegal, requiring all oil to packed in plastic or aluminum. This shut
down the tiny ghanis, or cold press mills. It destroyed the market for
our various oilseeds: mustard, linseed, sesame, groundnut and co-
conut. This coup by the edible oil industry has affected 10,000,000
million livelihoods. The substitution of atta, or flour, by packaged
and branded flour will influence 100,000,000 people. These millions are being pushed into a new poverty. Moreover, compulsory
packaging will produce an environmental burden of millions of tons
of plastic and aluminum.

The globalization of the food system is destroying the diversity of
local food cultures and local food economies. A global monoculture
is being forced on people by classifying everything that is fresh, local and handmade as health hazards. Human hands are being defined as the worst contaminants, and work for human hands is be-

*Nepal. Photos Richard Powers and Nuk Wheeler, Corbis/Grazia Neri*

ing outlawed, to be replaced by machines and chemicals bought from global corporations. These are not recipes for feeding the world, but ways of stealing livelihoods from the poor to create markets for the powerful.

**Biopiracy**

Women farmers in the Third World are mainly small-scale. They provide the basis of food security, and they provide food security in partnership with other species. The partnership between women and biodiversity has kept the world fed through history, feeds it at present, and will do so in the future. It is this partnership that needs to be preserved and promoted to ensure food security. Agriculture based on diversity, decentralization and improving small farm productivity by ecological methods is a female-centered, nature-friendly agriculture. In this women-centered agriculture, knowledge is shared, other species and plants are kin, not property, and sustainability is based on renewal of the earth's fertility, the regeneration of biodiversity, and the richness of species on farms to provide farm-grown inputs. In our paradigms, there is no place for monocultures of genetically engineered crops and monopolies of intellectual property rights (IPR) to seeds.

Monocultures and monopolies are emblematic of the male-dominated focus in agriculture. The war mentality underpinning armed forces and industry is evident from the names given to herbicides that destroy the economic basis of the survival of the poorest women in the rural areas of the Third World. Monsanto's herbicides are called 'Roundup', 'Machete' and 'Lasso'. American Home Products, which has merged with Monsanto, calls its herbicides 'Pentagon', 'Prowl', 'Scepter', 'Squadron', 'Cadre', 'Lightening', 'Assert' and 'Avenge'. This is the language of war, not sustainability. Sustainability is based on peace with the earth. The violence intrinsic to methods and metaphors used by global agribusiness and biotechnology corporations is a violence against nature's biodiversity and women's expertise and productivity. The violence intrinsic to the destruction of diversity through monocultures and the destruction of the freedom to save and exchange seeds through IPR monopolies is inconsistent with women's various nonviolent ways of interacting with nature and providing food security. This diversity of knowledge systems and production systems is the way forward to ensure that Third World women continue to play a central role as depositories of knowledge, producers and providers of food.

*India. Photo Joe McDonald. Tanzania. Photo David Turnley, Corbis/Grazia Neri*

One of the varieties we conserve and grow at the Navdanya farm in Doon Valley is the famous Basmati rice. This rice, which women farmers like Bija Devi, have been growing in my valley for centuries, is today being claimed as the recent invention of a novel type of rice by a US Corporation called RiceTec (patent no. 5,663, 454). The neem that our forebears used for centuries as a pesticide and fungicide has been patented for these uses by WR Grace, another US corporation. We have challenged Grace's patent at the European Patent Office, with the European Parliament Greens.

Biopiracy, by which western corporations steal centuries of collective knowledge and innovation carried out by Third World women, is now reaching epidemic proportions. It is now being justified by Monsanto in the guise of a 'partnership' between agribusiness and Third World women. For us, theft cannot be the basis of partnership. Partnership implies equality and mutual respect. This means that there is no room for biopiracy: those who have engaged in such piracy should apologize to those they have stolen from and whose intellectual and natural creativity they want to undermine through IPR monopolies. Partnership with Third World women requires changes to the WTO-TRIPs agreement that protects the pirates and punishes the original innovators, as in the case of the US-India TRIPs dispute. It will also involve changes in the US Patent Act, which allows the blatant theft of our biodiversity-related knowledge. These changes are essential to ensure that collective knowledge and innovation is protected and women are recognized and respected as depositaries of knowledge and biodiversity experts.

Women farmers have been the seed keepers and seed growers for millennia. Basmati is just one of 100,000 varieties of rice developed by Indian farmers. Diversity and perpetuity are the main features of our seed culture. In Central India, which is the Vavilov center for rice diversity, at the beginning of the agricultural season, farmers gather before the village deity, offer their varieties of rice and then share the seeds. This annual festival of Akti reaffirms the duty of saving and sharing seed among farming communities. It establishes partnership among farmers and with the earth.

IPRs on seeds are however criminalizing this duty to the earth and to each other by making seed saving and seed exchange illegal. The attempt to prevent farmers from saving seed is not just being made through the new genetic engineering technologies. Delta and Pine Land, now owned by Monsanto, and the US Department of Agriculture (USDA) have established new partnership through a jointly held patent (no. 5,723,785) for seed which has been genetically engineered to ensure that it does not germinate on harvest, thus forcing farmers to buy seed at each planting season. Termination of germination is a means for capital accumulation and market expansion. However, abundance in nature and for farmers shrinks as markets grow for Monsanto. When we sow seed, we pray, "May this seed be inexhaustible". Monsanto and the USDA on the other hand are saying, "Let this seed be terminated so that our profits and monopoly are inexhaustible". There can be no partnership between the terminator logic that destroys nature's renewability and the commitment to continuity of life held by women farmers of the Third World. The two worldviews do not merely clash. They are mutually exclusive. There can be no partnership between the logic of death on which Monsanto bases its expanding empire and the logic of life on which women farmers in the Third World base their partnership with the earth to provide food security for their families and communities. Genetic engineering and IPRs will rob Third World women and impoverish their creativity, innovation and decision-making power in agriculture. Instead of women deciding what is grown in fields and served in kitchens, agriculture based on globalization, genetic engineering and corporate monopolies on seeds will establish a food system and worldview in which the men in charge of global corporations control what is grown in our fields and what we eat. Corporate executives investing capital in theft and biopiracy will pose as the givers and owners of life. We will not be partners in this violent usurpation of the creativity of nature and Third World women by global biotechnology corporations. Calling themselves life sciences industry, they push millions of species and millions of small farmers closer to extinction.

*Mongolia, Morocco.*
*Photos Bruno Barbey, Magnum*

And it is not just other species, but the females of the human species that are being pushed to extinction. The violence unleashed by the Green Revolution and new agricultural technologies is also evident in the emergence and growth of female feticide in Punjab, the home of the Green Revolution. I first noted this connection in *Staying Alive*. The prosperous North Western States have only 17 percent of India's population but account for 80 percent of its female feticides. The juvenile sex ratio has dropped to 927 girls for every 1000 boys, indicating that 250,000 female feticides take place every year. I wrote in *Staying Alive* that women were becoming the disposable sex in a world where cash is the only measure of worth. Of women, as of everything else.

The future of biodiversity and the future of food security rests on
bringing women and small farmers back to the center of food
systems. Women live by the culture of conservation and sharing.
The world can be fed only by nourishing all the world's creatures. By giving food to other creatures and other species, we
maintain conditions for our own food security. By feeding the
earthworms, we feed ourselves. By feeding cows, we feed the soil
and in providing food for the soil, we provide food for humans.
This worldview of abundance is based on sharing and on a deep
awareness of humans as members of the earth's great family.
Awareness that, in impoverishing other beings, we impoverish
ourselves, and in nourishing other beings, we nourish ourselves.
That is the basis of sustainability. It was to defend biodiversity
and protect women's creativity and knowledge that I set up Navdanya in India. We have also initiated a global movement, Di-
verse Women for Diversity, for the safeguarding of biological and
cultural diversity. Without diversity there can be no peace, no
sustainability and no justice.

*Poland. Photo Raymond Gehman, Corbis/Grazia Neri*

*Cambogia. Photo Richard T Nowitz. India. Photo Lindsay Hebberd, Turks and Caicos Islands. Photo Phil Schermeister, Corbis/Grazia Neri*

# The Amal Cooperative

**I**n Arabic, amal means 'hope'. Hope is something the women of Tamanar have needed a lot of in recent years. Their village lies halfway between the imposing ramparts of ancient Essaouira, built high over the Atlantic by the Portuguese, and Agadir, the modern tourism-oriented city. The activity of the Amal Cooperative in Tamanar is based on the argan tree (*Argania Spinosa*, a member of the Sapotaceae), a species native to Morocco, which only grows in the arid zone along the Atlantic coast extending from Safi in the north to Goulimine to the south. This area is mainly inhabited by Berbers, the original people of Morocco.
The cooperative produces a great delicacy, argan oil, extracting it from the kernel of the stone in the argan tree fruit.

**Africa, Morocco, Tamanar**

### Zoubida and the others

The driving force of Amal has been Professor Zoubida Charrouf, a lecturer in chemistry at the Science Faculty of Mohammed V University in Rabat, as well as an international authority on the argan tree. In 1995, she drew up and presented to the local authorities a project to develop and promote argan oil, with the aim of conserving forests and improving conditions for rural Moroccan women. Helping her have been Khadija Ghalimi, who has studied business and marketing, and Amina Idalkadi, with a degree specializing in information technology and marketing and business management studies in Israel, now respectively director and president of the cooperative. They are the project's real driving force and the focus for all the cooperative's mem-

*Khadija Ghalimi and Amina Idalkadi*

bers. Khadija is responsible for management, organizing attendance at fairs and exhibitions and public relations. Amina helps her run the business, guides visitors round the project, where she explains the production process and supervises training for the women workers.

When it was first proposed to set up a cooperative, reactions were disappointing. The idea made the men in the village smile and puzzled local administrators, who had no confidence at all in a project entirely run by females.

Furthermore, the local administration would not grant permission for a site, the men did not intend to allow their wives to work and there was no public transport running from the countryside to the village.

However, the determined Zoubida managed to find support for the enterprise: the British Embassy and Consulate and the Comité d'Entraide Internationale (Committee for International Co-operation) funded the purchase of the equipment needed.

One year after presenting the first proposal, funds were available and so were women workers. Only premises had still to be found.

Although the situation at Tamanar had come to a standstill, Professor Charrouf decided to set up two other women's cooperatives for argan in the same region: at Tizdi (opened in 1998) and Mesti (2000). They, too, were funded in part by foreign and Moroccan organizations.

The attitude of the men of Tamanar gradually began to change as they realized that the cooperative would bring extra income into families and there would also be a beneficial impact on tourism. The local authority finally made a site available and Amal commenced operations in March 1999. There were 16 pioneers in the venture, led by Khadija Ghalimi and Amina Idalkadi. Today the cooperative employs 47 members full-time, mainly widows or divorcées aged from 25 to 60. Paradoxically, it is this social isolation, as well as their need of cash, which enables them to enjoy the 'privilege' of working. Married women, who are accepted by the community, are not normally permitted by their husbands to go out to work.

## Argan, ecology and development

The argan tree originated in the Tertiary period. It grows, only in Morocco, at altitudes of 400 to 500 meters, with the wild olive. It is very hardy, resistant to heat, and survives well in the poor, arid soil of what in Morocco is called the 'argan forest', an area extending over about 800,000 hectares from Safi to Goulimine in the southwest of the country. Manufacturing and other argan-related activities support at least 3,000,000 people, discouraging population drift away from rural regions and contributing to environmental balance in the area. Argan wood is used as fuel or for carpentry, the leaves and pulp of the fruit feed goats and camels, oil is obtained from the kernels, the nutshells provide more fuel and the pressed residues from the kernels are excellent fodder for livestock. In addition, the roots of the argan metabolize salts that are important for soil fertility and, obviously, protect the soil from erosion by water and wind.

But the argan forest of about 20,000,000 trees is under serious threat from desertification affecting the whole Mediterranean area. Extreme drought and intensive exploitation of the forest have resulted in about a third disappearing in the course of the last century and recent studies indicate that about 40 percent of the present area could be lost by 2008.

The poverty of the region's inhabitants has led to shortsighted exploitation of the argan, which is practically the only resource. The greatest damage has been caused by sheep and goats: the latter here literally climb up into the trees, reaching even the tallest ones 8 to 10 meters of the ground, and devour leaves, branches and new shoots. Neither are the locals averse to cutting down trees for firewood, or to clear the area for more profitable crops in the short term, such as barley and cereals. The government is attempting to tackle this critical situation by implementing national reforestation campaigns and programs for the protection of the forest heritage. The Minister for Water and Forests has also taken steps to protect the argan from human destruction by fencing off entire areas of forest in the province of Essaouira. The argan can live for centuries and has great economic, ecological and social value. That is why much of the 'arganeraie', the argan-growing area, has since 1998 been classified as a Biosphere Reserve by UNESCO to save the tree and meet the needs of the rural population.

## Food and cosmetics

The Amal cooperative processes about 300 tonnes of fruit a year, which is picked by families during the two months when it is ripe, in July and August. But is purchased regularly over the whole year by the cooperative's agent (he is the only man who works for Amal: women cannot make purchases at the market). This steady source of income is making families realize how important it is to protect the argan trees, which, even when growing on private land, are still public property. To ensure there is a good harvest to sell to the cooperative, the residents are beginning, as best they can, to protect the trees from animals. Instead of eating fruit and shoots, the animals can feed on waste from oil processing.

The cooperative owns of the Targanine brand, taken from the name of the umbrella project for the three cooperatives set up by Professor Charrouf. It is used for two different product lines, a range of food products from roasted kernels and cosmetics from raw kernels. The main food product is Arganati edible oil, which has a golden color and nutty flavor. It is a staple ingredient of Berber cuisine, used in couscous, meat tajine, fish, salad or simply spread on bread. This oil has obtained certification as an arganic food product from the Qualité France authority and can be sold as '100 percent natural oil'. Then there is Amlou Beldi, a cream made from almonds, honey and argan oil, which is spread on bread. The cosmetics line contains Arganium beauty serum, obtained from pressed raw kernels, which has healing, moisturizing and tonic properties for skin, hair and nails.

About 80 percent of the cooperative's production is sold directly at the factory door. Locals also purchase the beauty serum, since edible oil is a common homemade product, but tourists – guided tours are organized at Amal, which brings money into the whole village – are keen purchasers of edible oil and Amlou Beldi. The remaining 20 percent is distributed to outlets in the main Moroccan cities and goods are also shipped abroad to order, especially to Europe and the US. The cosmetic oil is bought wholesale by foreign manufacturers of beauty products.

The cooperative purchases dried fruit at local markets every two weeks. After further drying, the fruit is transferred to the pulping machine before being cleaned again and checked by the women. The nuts are now opened manually to extract the kernels, which are roasted in a gas roaster. They are then left overnight to cool and transferred to a mechanical press, which gives twice the yield of pressing by hand. The oil is then filtered and bottled, with nitrogen to prevent oxidation. The product may be conserved for 24 months.

Manual extraction of the oil is a very long process, involving about 20 hours' work for a single liter, and is done in the home by just one woman. The kernels are first ground to a paste and a small quantity of luke-warm water added to facilitate extraction of the oil when the paste is pressed in the hands. The oil is then poured into recycled plastic bottles and used for personal consumption or sold by the roadside. But home-made oil has poorer sensory characteristics, is of inferior quality, does not keep so well and is oxidizes quickly.

## A social role

In addition to the 47 members who work at the main plant, the cooperative has another 120 women working for it part-time from home, either because they live a long way from the village or because their husbands refuse to let them to leave the home to go to work. The fee for membership of Amal is 200 dirham, about USD 17, or 5 kg of kernels. Every two weeks, the argan kernels that each women has shelled are weighed and they are paid for their work: 35 dirham, or about USD 3, per kilo of kernels.

All the workers involved in shelling the kernels are paid on a piecework basis while some members, those involved in roasting, pressing and filtering, bottling, labeling and packing, receive a daily wage of 35 dirham.

Ten percent of the cooperative's profit is shared among. Turnover for 1999-2000 was 537,235 dirham, the equivalent of about USD 45,000.

The women are proud to work for the cooperative. They feel respected and their monthly pay of around USD 50-75 allows them to send their children to school, improve their living conditions, eat better and look after themselves. The cooperative is a way of achieving independence and escaping from their isolation. The government also organizes a weekly literacy course for the cooperative and a public child-care facility next to Amal looks after the workers' children. The cooperative also expects every member to open a savings account and make regular deposits of at least 25 dirham, or USD 2.

**Motives for Slow Food Award**

A project which combines the protection of an extraordinary tree like the argan, quality production and the emancipation of Berber women in the rural Souss region might look like a pipe-dream. The Amal cooperative in Tamanar, with founder Zoubida Charrouf, Khadija Ghalimi and Amina Idalkadi, who helped Charrouf give a practical form to her idea, and the dozens of women working there, is well on the way to making that dream come true. There were difficulties in setting it up and there may be further problems to come. But thanks to these women, a piece of woodland will be saved and the Berber people will still be able use the argan tree, perhaps one of Morocco's oldest inhabitants.

Special Jury Award

*Alessandra Abbona*

# Doña Sebastiana Juárez Broca

**D**oña Sebastiana Juárez Broca was born on 23 January 1949 in Guayo 1<sup>era</sup> Sección, a poor village in the Comalcalco district, about 50 kilometers from Villahermosa in the Mexican state of Tabasco. She has always worked on the land while also looking after her family, husband, Don Asunción de La Cruz Hérnandez, and their 13 children. Her formal education stopped at elementary school. Doña Sebastiana has always stood out amongst the small farmers of Comalcalco for her social and religious activism, and she is a leading figure in the community. Her greatest quality is her determination, which has enabled her to cope with the hard life of a peasant farmer, juggling work in the fields and family.

### America, Mexico, Tabasco, Comalcalco

**Tabasco – cocoa and oil**

Tabasco is a very fertile, mainly flat region in the south east of the country on the Gulf of Mexico. It was here that Hernán Cortez landed and cocoa was discovered with the new continent. Tabasco, particularly the region of Chontalpa which includes Comalcalco, is in fact the first place in the world where cocoa was cultivated: nowhere else on the planet is so intimately connected to the crop. It was the Mayas who worked out how to grow cocoa, which has its biological origins in Amazonia.

Cocoa was held in high regard by pre-Columbian cultures, so much so that cocoa beans, after they had been being washed and hardened by being danced on according to a well-defined ritual, were used as currency. Consumption of cocoa as a food was limited to a privileged few, however. The Spaniards were immediately interested in this product and decided to export it to all their colonies, which led to its spreading all over the world.

Tabasco produces 80 percent of Mexican cocoa. In past times, the crop was grown throughout the country but over the years, it has gradually concentrated in the southeast. The remaining 20 percent of national production comes from nearby Chiapas. There are 22,000 Tabascan families who make their living from cocoa but since the 1960s, the cocoa economy has gone into recession. Government policies, far from helping small farmers, have completely undermined the cultivation system. The formation of the National Union of Cocoa Producers literally ruined the lives of small farmers, plunging them into poverty. The Union was created to collect green cocoa from producers, dry it and then sell it to exporters. Harvesting takes place during the rainy season so the sun cannot be relied on to dry the crop. Expensive gas-fired equipment is needed. Small farmers cannot afford driers and so depend on whoever owns it. The services of the Union, which has offices in the main towns, soon proved to be an unbearable burden. Prices for green cocoa were fixed at very low levels and cor-

rupt officials bled the Union of the cash required to pay the producers on time. Cocoa growers initially just received an undertaking to pay, which had to be cashed at the Union offices, but four or five costly visits would be necessary before they actually obtained what they were owed. At the end of the procedure, much of the money had been spent on transport and little was left to provide for the family. The difficult life that growers had to contend with was not improved when the so-called 'coyotes' appeared as intermediaries. The nickname the farmers gave to these intermediaries of the multinationals is significant: operating from a position of greater financial strength, the coyotes paid immediately but gave a much lower price. That is where we are today. A kilogram of cocoa beans sells for around eight or nine pesos (about USD 1). With an annual yield of 700 kilograms per hectare and an average farm size of 1.5 to 2 hectares, the annual income of a cocoa-farming family is about 12,000 pesos, equivalent to about USD 1,300. This income is nothing like sufficient for the generally large families involved.

With problems like this, it is easy to understand why farmers have abandoned the land. They swell the masses of desperate people emigrating to the Federal District of Mexico City, or finding work in

Villahermosa, an oil-drilling town. Oil was discovered in the 1960s and fast became a new source of wealth for the few, and of exploitation for those who cannot survive by working on the land. The oil industry also has a huge impact on the environment. It is thought that at the present rate, cocoa might be abandoned entirely in a few years, with damaging consequences for the forests in the region.

## Organic farming for the Mayas' chocolate

Doña Sebastiana and her husband refused to accept the situation and have always tried to provide for their children in ways that did not require them to leave the land. In 1984, they foresaw that organic farming could be a way of adding value to their crop while enabling cost savings in cultivation. But they had no way of selling organic cocoa in a market controlled by large companies. In addition, government authorities were strongly opposed to their venture, which attempted to involve their whole community. The local authorities in Tabasco, have always supported the coyotes, who have never been shy about buying favors. That was why the idea of Doña Sebastiana and her husband was not immediately successful.

However in 1993, they met Alma Rosa Garcés Medina and Mariano Gutiérrez Aparicio, two biologists who had decided to move to Tabasco to offer resources and support to small farmers in difficulty. The two biologists were working on a project to produce organically farmed cocoa and had access to financial help from the Dutch-based NOVIB organization, which certifies and trades organic produce throughout the world. Doña Sebastiana – or Tia Tana, as she is affectionately known in the community – and four other women decided to process the organic cocoa grown by her husband in the traditional manner of the women of Tabasco and, before them, of Mayan women. Doña Sebastiana began to use some of the family's crop to make chocolate to sell to tourists in hotels and at Villahermosa airport. The idea was a winner. First of all, it involved the women in the family's work, giving them a more active role. Moreover, processed chocolate could be sold at a much higher price (60 pesos a kilo, compared to eight for cocoa beans). In 1997, Alma Rosa and Mariano decided to form a non-profit association, the Asesoría Tecnica en Cultivos Organicos, or Technical Advisory Service for Organic Crops, to promote a complex cocoa-farming project that could involve both men and women. The men would be responsible for the land, producing organic cocoa and developing a system of reforestation, which would recreate the ideal conditions of shade for growing the crop. The women, thanks to Doña Sebastiana's initiative, would produce chocolate in the traditional manner. In this way, the added value of the organic crop and processed chocolate would boost family earnings and make it possible to purchase drying equipment. Doña Sebastiana immediately joined in enthusiastically, working hard, using her strong personality and the respect she enjoyed in the community to get as many farmers as possible involved in the project. The result is that today there are seven cooperatives, four men's and three women's, all working on the project. They are known as SSS, or 'sociedades de solidaridad social'. The first, in honor of the person who provided the decisive impetus, is called Chocolate Tia Tana. They cover almost the entire Chontalpa district and involve 1,104 members or relatives of members. The following objectives have still to be achieved: the creation of groups formed of one male SSS and one female for processing; the organic certification of all the SSS; obtaining processing equipment for all the cooperatives (at present, there is only one drying plant).

**Tia Tana's lesson**

Until a short time ago, cocoa produced by farmers was almost entirely sold as beans for a swift cash return. The small amount kept back for personal consumption was used to make pozol, a high-energy drink based on cocoa, maize and water, which still helps farmers to resist the humid heat of the region. The need to quickly sell their entire harvest meant that the traditional method of making chocolate, which was carried out by women, had been almost completely forgotten. Doña Sebastiana saw how important this work could be for the women of Tabasco: it is an activity that binds women's work to the family, increases household income and provides an alternative to emigration.

There are three women's cooperatives: Chocolate Tia Tana, with 15 members from Comalcalco; Grupo de Mujeres La Guadalupa, which has 23 members from Cárdenas; and Grupo de Mujeres La Carmelitas, with 32 members, again from Cárdenas. Today, they process the chocolate and sell it in attractive jute bags. All production is manual and, for now, accounts for only a small part of total cocoa production since market outlets have not yet been developed.

Green cocoa is first of all stored for between seven and ten days, depending on air humidity. During this period it ferments, which releases its fragrances and develops its sensory characteristics. It is then dried. Next, the beans are shaken in glass bottles to remove the outer husk, which is discarded. At this point, the cocoa can be roasted on a wood fire, using large, flat metal containers and plates, and is then ready to be turned into chocolate. The beans are ground four or five times using small hand grinders until they reach the desired fineness. An ingredient is added at each stage: cane sugar, cinnamon, milk and a pinch of pepper. It is important to remember that this chocolate is made using whole cocoa since the whole bean is used. In contrast, industrial processes frequently separate the fat, which is the most nutritious, flavorsome and fragrant component, to be used in for cosmetics or medicines. The final product is shaped into nuggets or doubloons: they are delicious to eat as they are but they can also be dissolved in boiling milk to make a good hot chocolate drink.

The four men's cooperatives are General Fco. J. Mújica with 28 members at Cárdenas; Lic. José Ma. Pino Suárez, which has 32 members in Cunduacán; Esperanza del C-11 with 30 members at Cárdenas; and finally Costa del Tabasco, with 16 members at Comalcalco. Costa del Tabasco was the first to be set up and it has its own drying equipment. Doña Sebastiana's husband is a member and from next year it will produce about 300 ton of certified organic cocoa.

The men's cooperatives perform a very important ecological function. In addition to farming organically, they are also implementing a program of reforestation. Cocoa needs shade and so there have to be taller trees in the plantation. This system assures the conservation of the Tabasco ecosystem but was about to be abandoned. In desperation, farmers were cutting down the tallest trees to earn a little cash from the wood. Today, the cooperatives are carrying out a 'progressive level' reforestation plan. In this system, trees that grow tall very quickly are planted together with trees that grow much more slowly. It is thus possible to assure shade for many years and at the same time benefit from the trees that grow quickly. Timber is obviously important but the trees provide tropical flowers and fruit, which the women preserve and sell with the chocolate.

*Carlo Bogliotti*

---

**Motives for Slow Food Award**

Doña Sebastiana Juárez Broca is an emblematic figure in her community. She has always worked to defend cocoa growing by small farmers and to make it profitable. Her role as organizer in the community, and her farsightedness in accepting help and advice from impartial and strongly motivated people make her a key figure in the emancipation of women in Tabasco. She has been able to rescue and disseminate knowledge of traditional processing methods for chocolate, providing an opportunity to earn money and play an active part in society. Doña Sebastiana's endeavors have enabled the men to finance their project for organic, environment-friendly cultivation and to shake off the impositions of intermediaries who fix ludicrously low prices for the raw commodity. This small woman farmer from Tabasco transformed a world threatened by poverty, exploitation, pollution and corruption. High quality cocoa from Tabasco has provided a way out. It is necessary to support the projects in the long-term so that they may serve as a model for the whole state and the end product can be accepted and a just price obtained in the international market.

*Special Jury Award*

# Adriana Valcarcel

**A**driana Valcarcel Manga, 40, is a chemistry graduate and runs a company that produces flour, baked pastries, puffed cereals and herbal teas based on traditional Andean products. She comes from a middle-class family. Her father worked for a state brewery until his retirement and her mother looked after the house and four children. Adriana is the eldest. One of her sisters, also a chemist, teaches, her brother is a hydraulic engineer and her other sister is a doctor.

## America, Peru, Cuzco

### Mara and the return of amaranth

Adriana graduated in 1985 and moved from Cuzco to Trujillo to do her training in a food canning company. She was placed in quality control with the job of measuring levels of acidity in canned tomatoes. She knew at once that she would not remain with the company a moment longer than necessary. It refused to believe that her working life would simply be a matter of taking measurements. She finished her training but turned down the invitation to continue working for the company. Yet the food industry continued to attract her. She spoke about it with her uncle and aunt, who she was staying with in Trujillo, and they encouraged her. She started out by preparing food, such as fried platanos, a type of banana, which she sold in the street. The scheme had some success, she enjoyed it and managed to save a little money, but did not yet have a clear idea of a definite project.

Then all at once the amaranth boom arrived in Peru. It became fashionable with intellectuals and there were research projects, articles and studies. Adriana began to get interested too, and even enthusiastic. Amaranth was what she would get involved in, but she wanted to produce it, not do research. She contacted some friends in Cuzco and proposed the idea of setting up a company to process amaranth. Adriana and her friends managed to put together enough money to start up the company, Aroma, which was already in production at the end of 1986, even though it was not officially set up until 3 February 1987. There were three women and a man, all chemists, but with very limited knowledge of agriculture. Adriana worked during the day and enrolled in an evening course on Andean agriculture. They also had to find suppliers for the raw material. There were not many as amaranth had been on the point of extinction before the new surge of interest appeared. They eventually located the most suitable region and found reliable growers. In the meantime PRONAK, the Programa Nacional de la Kiwicha, had been set up - kiwicha is the Peruvian Indian term for amaranth - and they were able to get advice. That was how Adriana Valcarcel's adventures in food production began. The early years were far from easy. She and her friends were working in unsuitable premises and had to do everything themselves, from purchasing amaranth to arranging delivery. Her family, who watched her work herself to into the ground for no financial return, disapproved and were unsupportive. The company changed over time, her friends went in other directions, new partners arrived and then left again. Today, Adriana is the sole owner of Mara. Even the name has changed since she and her partners soon realized that Aroma did not project the image they were trying to create. In the Aymara and Quechua languages, mara means 'enduring' and this was the concept they wanted to express. They were not simply producing something to eat: their products offered more than a flavor; they were the continuation of an age-old culture.

The first two products were toasted amaranth and toasted amaranth flour. But there were differing market responses: mothers and grandmothers knew that it was a healthy, nutritious, high-energy product, and were delighted that they could buy it again, but younger people preferred foods that were more modern. It was therefore necessary to make the amaranth desirable to young people. That is how the third product in the amaranth line was born: confite, or grains of puffed amaranth coated in naturally colored sugar. Now amaranth really took off, appearing on cakes, in yogurt, in fruit salad, on biscuits and on ice cream.

The year of the turnaround was 1995. At a time when the company was beginning to be successful, but was involved in a major dispute with the tax authorities, which it would win, Adriana was awarded a scholarship to study in Belgium. She did not feel she could go away – losing the tax case would have meant closing down the company – but the opportunity was too tempting. Her father, by now retired, told her he would look after the company in the weeks while she was away. It was the first time he had manifested approval of any kind for his daughter's work and Adriana managed to swallow her pride and accept the offer. On her return from Belgium, she found her father enthusiastic and involved with the work. Since then, he has worked full-time for Mara, receiving a salary. Another battle had been won, simply by using the weapons of work and patience. Adriana never broke with her family. She always lived with her parents, as is usual in Peru for an unmarried woman. "Of course, it is very convenient. My mother is a traditionalist. She has never worked outside the home and has always looked after us children so we

## Motives for Slow Food Award

Know the past. Live in the present. Keeping a close eye on the future. Adriana Valcarcel has based her choices on the concepts of identity and diversification, reaffirming and renewing her links with Native American culture. Convinced of the importance of these two concepts, she has created a productive and profitable enterprise, enabling her to revive amaranth, an almost abandoned crop, and to create jobs that provide security and dignity. Her entrepreneurial activity is a model for development in a country that still hovers between extreme poverty and a pursuit of modernization that ignores existing equilibria and the needs of the weakest.

never had to worry about cooking or keeping the house tidy. I have learned to cook the things I produce, but only in the last few years. Still, the reason I never thought about leaving is that I never wanted a hostile situation. I didn't want a split or slammed doors. I couldn't accept their negative response. I wasn't doing anything wrong, just something new. That was what frightened them. But when my father had the chance to see at first hand what I was doing, he finally understood. And I was waiting for that moment".

### Identity and quality

This is the way Adriana Valcarcel thinks. When she says no, it is final. When she says yes, it is for life. She believes that when the right things are done well, they will sooner or later have the success they deserve. This slightly built woman may look frail but she's a steamroller. She has always known where she was going. There are dozens of photograph albums in her office that record every aspect of the business, with dates and captions. But the cataloguing is not a recent job. It was all done during the long struggle. You reach the company offices on the outskirts of Cuzco – a new move is imminent – along a dusty dirt road but inside is a piece of Switzerland. The HACCP (hazard analysis and critical control point) system is observed to the last comma, workers are neatly dressed and working spaces practical. Everything is planned, from washing the

wheels of trucks entering the yard to birthday messages posted on the notice board for staff. There are 12 people working there full-time and 30-35 seasonal workers. A notice encourages everyone to get involved, "If you're not part of the solution, you're part of the problem".

The range of products has now expanded considerably. There are bars of chocolate, amaranth and honey, amaranth biscuits, amaranth and quinoa flour, muesli, toasted maize … and everything is available in individual portions for the tourists who tackle the Camino Real, the magnificent trek which leads from Cuzco to Macchu Picchu. The labels have also been designed with care. "We must have an attractive Peruvian image. We can't have our products conforming to the US style of packaging. We are different but there is no reason for our products to be any less attractive. In fact, it's when we try to copy the US style that we turn out our worst results". Sales in 1987 totaled about USD 100. Last year, turnover was roughly USD 200,000. Mara products are sold in the shops of Cuzco and in a Lima supermarket chain with 25 outlets. Exports started in 1996 but Peru's reputation in foreign markets has deteriorated so badly in the past two years that demand for goods has dried up. In addition, for the last four years Mara has won government contracts to supply biscuits enriched with iron, vitamins and minerals to state schools in the poorest parts of the country.

This comes to about 40,000 portions of 90 grams per day over the whole school year, a contract that represents a significant professional achievement as well as a big production commitment.

One of Mara's key strategies to stay in the market is the introduction of new products. Mara cannot compete with the products large companies have been selling for years and which have an established market. Their other strong suit is quality. Mara products have obtained organic certification from the Dutch Skal organization. Amaranth, like quinoa, has had to shake off its image as a food of the poor. Today, natural products are prestigious, but you have to know how to produce and market them.

## A rural school of ecology

These are the stakes: new, attractive, healthful products made from traditional local raw materials that communicate an identity. Not only does Adriana Valcarcel remember these roots, she is actually trying to promote. That's why Mara and two other companies, one a fruit and vegetable processor, the other a condiment, herb and spice producer, have formed the ProCuzco Association, which has bought five hectares of land about an hour's drive from town. A small farm has been set up where many varieties of maize, herbs, vegetables and fruit are grown experimentally, guinea pigs are raised and eucalyptus honey produced. But the most important project has been launched with the local community, numbering about 200 families. The ProCuzco Association, in collaboration with a US-based NGO, USAID, has set up a rural ecological school to teach the basics of agriculture no longer taught in the home. As families were unable to earn a living, they had almost stopped farming the land they owned. The ProCuzco Association has started to get children involved in a school of agriculture, holding lessons at the farm but with practical work to do at home. The children have involved their families, first by obtaining a small allotment for themselves. Then, when the parents saw their children's enthusiasm, what they were growing and of course that they were earning money – ProCuzco purchased the crop – the grown-ups began to take part, too. There are now 75 families growing food. The three companies supply the peasant farmers with seed and then purchase the harvest. Furthermore, thanks to external funding from an association of Peruvians resident in the US, ten computers have been installed at the farm and the children have quickly learned how to use them. They go to the farm after school whenever they want, to 'play' on the computer, socializing, interacting with the world and growing up. Preserving the identity of Peruvian Indian communities also means preserving the physical locations where those communities live. If young people leave, if they cannot find something interesting to do, the communities will become ghost towns. It is in this way that the Internet and a computer can be tools to bind individuals to their culture instead of deracinating them. Young people remain, villages gel, produce and find market opportunities. There is a return to growing things but they are grown better, following the guidelines of organic agriculture. People learn to make compost and to separate wastes.

"The third millennium," says Adriana, "has now arrived for Native Americans. We are all a mixture of different civilizations, Aymara, Tiahuanaco and Inca, as well as Western culture. It doesn't make sense to separate one out and preserve it in a museum. The world evolves through interaction and new solutions. The resentment that the defenders of Andean cultures have nurtured towards the Spanish doesn't have any sense. Every people in the world, every country has been invaded. Why should America have stayed immune to this phenomenon? Sure, crimes were committed but this happened wherever there was conquest. If the Spanish hadn't done, it then someone else would have. We are now what we are, a mixture of everything that has passed through, like Europeans or Asians. What good does resentment do? On the contrary, we should be happy that the Andean culture still survives and can teach us so many things. But presuming to create oases of Andean purity would be crazy, a sterile anachronism".

*C. S.*

# Bija Devi

**B**ija Devi was born 54 years ago at Lostu Badi-Bargad, a small village in Garhwal, the Himalayan region in the west of the state of Uttar Anchal. She has worked as a farmer since she was seven, and working on the land prevented her from attending school. She married at 13 and, when she was about 20, moved with her husband and two small children to the town of Dehra Dun, where for about 20 years she led the life of a homemaker. However, she always found time for her small vegetable garden. When her children left school and became independent, Bija had more free time and through a friend met the family of Vandana Shiva, whom she asked for employment as a servant. Vandana Shiva is a world famous authority in the environmental field who has published various studies on the problem of intellectual property rights, genetically modified organisms and sustainable agriculture. In 1993, she was awarded the Alternative Nobel Prize.

Vandana Shiva was planning a project for the conservation and exchange of seeds, which became the Navdanya program, and asked Bija Devi to look after another vegetable garden, this time at Shiva's house, where the first seeds collected from Garhwal farmers were planted. Although she has experienced difficult times, particularly in recent years (her husband died of cancer a few years ago and

**she had a serious car accident in 1999), Bija has managed to carry out her work with passion and cheerfulness, infecting her co-workers and the farmers who have joined the movement with her ever-present childlike smile. It has been a relatively small step from the vegetable garden, via a modest plot of land, to the splendid Navdanya farm, which Bija Devi now manages. Ten years have sufficed to bring about this small Indian miracle.**

## Asia, India, Dehra Dun, Uttar Anchal

### The Navdanya movement

The name Navdanya means 'nine seeds' in Hindi. It was inspired by the widespread custom in the south of India of planting nine seeds in a pot on the first day of the year. The women carry the pots to the river after nine days so they can meet and compare results, observing which seeds have performed best. They then exchange seeds so that each family can plant the best seeds available during the planting season, thus optimizing food supplies in the village. The objectives of the Navdanya program are to protect biodiversity, to create a seed bank for the farmers in the movement so that they can exchange seeds and to convert fields to entirely organic agriculture, using exclusively organic fertilizers and pesticides. With her knowledge of varieties, storage and cultivation of seeds and her deep desire that the treasures of her country should not be lost, Bija Devi – Bija means 'seed', which makes her story all the more fascinating – perfectly embodies the philosophy of the movement. This enables her to put into practice all the principles that Navdanya affirms. During the association's early years, Bija and Shiva's work mainly consisted in meeting farmers in the area, beginning to collect seeds in danger of disappearing and trying to persuade the farmers to abandon chemical fertilizers and pesticides, which had been widely promoted by the Indian government in the 1950s to back up the so-called Green Revolution. Thanks to substantial technical and scientific knowledge (genetically selected plants, agricultural machinery, fertilizers and pesticides), food production was boosted to address the problem of feeding a growing population. The move had positive aspects but also caused large-scale degradation and pollution of the land and underground aquifers. Another drawback was the use of hybrid seeds, which for the first time made farmers dependent on manufacturing companies, upsetting the age-old equilibrium which had always enabled farmers to use seeds collected from one season to the next.

Focusing on the importance of safeguarding health and on the dangers associated with pesticides and fertilizers, Navdanya established personal contacts with the farmers in the Dehra Dun area (the movement is now also active in another five Indian states). Those contacted were involved in a radical three-year reconversion project, beginning with a small area of farmed land and working towards a complete shift from chemical to organic methods. Since local agriculture serves essentially for self-consumption, the farmers were highly motivated by a sense of pride in their own produce. This perception of quality had a positive effect on members of the movement and significantly influenced its expansion.

A further fundamental feature of the philosophy of the movement was the strong sense of belonging that was created among the farm-

ers. Money was saved on pesticides, fertilizers and seeds, a dependence-generating mechanism in the hands of the multinationals who, using near-usurious loan arrangements, have reduced an alarming number of Indian farmers to semi-slavery. Improved quality of the crops has meant that word of mouth has become the means by which Navdanya recruits new members. Family and neighborly relationships developed by villagers over the centuries can do more than organized efforts: weekly meetings and occasional visits are arranged by the coordinators of the movement to strengthen this sense of belonging and difference from farmers who have not yet moved over to sustainable farming.

One thing that the movement is focusing on at the present time is the direct sale of its produce. Navdanya has set up a stall at Dilli Haat, a New Delhi market where you can find everything from saris to crafts from the most remote parts of India. The program sells rice, lentils, juices and other produce from its farm or reconverted fields, thus providing the farmers with a first opportunity to earn a modest amount of money.

**The organic farm**

About six years ago, the work carried out by Navdanya focused on the creation of its organic farm. Under Bija Devi's leader-

ship, more than 600 types of vegetable are now grown. These include about 250 varieties of rice, of which 13 are Basmati, 19 varieties of corn, three of corn and four of lentils, as well as sesame, coriander, cumin, six types of mustard, peas, peppers and a large number of medicinal plants. No detail is neglected, from the plants used to reinforce the banks of the rice fields (the rains here can have a devastating effect) to the rotation system designed to optimize soil yield, the collection of urine from cattle (used as an insecticide) and the cultivation of a pulse used exclusively to improve the compost.

Bija's experience was handed down to her by her mother and mother-in-law, confirming that women are responsible for sowing, harvesting and storing, while it is up to the men to prepare the soil. This experience allows her to manage the complete plant growth cycle from seed to food. Bija selects the best seeds, decides which to plant and stores them according to traditional methods. She keeps the seeds in three different ways to make sure that at least one of them will be successful. The first batch is simply dried and put in a tin can, the second is mixed with ashes, and for the third, she moistens the jute sacks which will hold them with oil of Neem, a plant with strong healing and insect-repellent properties. After this, the sacks and cans are placed in the seed room, the inner sanctuary of the whole farm. "You have to take off your shoes before entering," explains Bija Devi, "because the seeds contain the secret of life. We worship them as a divine force".

Another of the great things that Bija has done is to reintroduce to the farm and to the farmers of Navdanya the ancient practice of growing 12 different species on the same small plot of land, rice, millet, peanuts, corn, mustard, mango and so on. This ensures that the soil is not depleted of specific substances, as happens with single-crop farming, and enables the farmer to have a varied crop. It is also extended over the season since the plants grow at different rates.

Finally, Bija Devi is an excellent cook and holds lessons for the women of the village, teaching at Navdanya workshops in India's cities, mainly Delhi and Madras. In this way, she contributes to the preservation and promulgation of Garhwal's rich culinary tradition.

*Nicola Ferrero*

---

**Motives for Slow Food Award**

Bija Devi and Navdanya's achievements in this region are extraordinary. In the valley around Dehra Dun, there are now more than 1,000 families involved in the movement and 34 hill villages that have completely reconverted to organic methods.

Bija and her co-workers organize seed exchanges with the farmers, hold weekly meetings and organize two large annual workshops. One is dedicated to the creation of compost and the other to learning about and using all-natural insecticides. The project is also about to take on a new, exciting challenge – a school (building is well advanced) where the basic principles of sustainable farming will be taught in collaboration with the Schumacher College, a veritable institution in the UK for organic agriculture.

The dedication and passion which Bija Devi brings to her work can be summed up, "I cannot forgive myself for wasting more than 20 years doing other things. Who knows how many other species I could have saved?"

Special Jury Award

# Marie-Noëlle Anderson

**M**arie-Noëlle Anderson, 55, lives in Geneva and works as a healer. She was born in Johannesburg, South Africa, in 1946 of a Swiss mother and South African father with a Scottish background. In her healing work, she is guided by the principles of traditional African medicine and has become a spokeswoman for, and popularizer of, the approach. She has also undertaken projects in collaboration with various NGOs to protect medicinal plants and preserve the traditional knowledge of healers in Africa.

She has inherited a love for nature, particularly the mountains, from her mother, with whom she moved to Switzerland when still a child. She had a business-oriented education but during her adolescence, her desire to know more about the country of her birth prompted her to make long visits to South Africa over about seven years. For political reasons, she did not return until 1991, the year after Nelson Mandela was released from prison.

In the meantime, she married, had a child and spent many years abroad, mainly in the US and Italy, where she was involved in various activities while developing her interest in the curative properties of plants. She then returned to Switzerland permanently, where she completed a four-year training course in Celtic traditions under the guidance of a French teacher.

Towards the end of the 1980s, Africa came back into her life when she was invited to visit a hospital
near Bulawayo in Zimbabwe, where doctors trained
in Western medicine worked alongside traditional
healers. She decided to devote herself to a fulltime
study of the methods of traditional African healing,
under the guidance of David Ngwenya of the ITHO
(International Traditional Healers Organization).
In addition to working as a healer in Geneva,
Marie-Noëlle Anderson organizes courses, training
and workshops in traditional African medicine.
She edits the *L'Arbre à Palabre* series of books on
African issues for the Swiss publisher Jouvence.
She is occasionally invited to share her experience with various institutions, such as the Univer-
sity of Geneva, Geneva Hospital and the European
School in Munich, Bavaria, and she also works
with organizations such as the WWF and Pro
Specie Rara, for whom she has organized chil-
dren's workshops on plants.

## Europe, Switzerland, Geneva

**Itho and medicinal plants**

The ITHO, or International Traditional
Healers Organization, is recognized
by the World Health Organization. It
was set up in Zimbabwe as the Tho
and subsequently became an international organization, promoting
awareness of HIV-related issues and
other illnesses. Among its members
are healers from Africa, mainly Zimbabwe, Botswana, Swaziland, Zam-
bia, South Africa and Malawi, Europe, America and Asia.

Traditional healers can meet West-
ern-trained doctors in workshops
organized by the ITHO and receive
from them basic information on the
measures necessary to combat the
illnesses that afflict Africa. Valuable
experience and information can be
exchanged in this way on issues
such as emergency treatment, fam-

ily planning, breast-feeding, cancer treatments, tuberculosis and HIV. Marie-Noëlle Anderson is the ITHO representative in Geneva and its liaison with Déclaration de Berne, the NGO that is drawing up a document for the protection of medicinal plants and the knowledge of traditional healers. The aim is to produce a document which can be added to the corpus of international law and provide a framework adaptable to the requirements of individual countries. Thanks to the support of Marie-Noëlle Anderson and her knowledge of medicinal plants, Déclaration de Berne works with the Global Intellectual Property Issues division of WIPO, the World Intellectual Property Organization, an international body based in Geneva, to ensure compliance with the Convention on Biodiversity in countries that have already signed it.

Unfortunately, large pharmaceutical companies and research laboratories are indiscriminately exploiting medicinal plants in many African countries, profiting from the knowledge of traditional healers who, driven by poverty, accept ridiculously low payments for their skills.

Traditional healers know the plants, what benefits they provide and how

### Motives for Slow Food Award

With her deep knowledge of the cultures and rhythms of the Dark Continent, Marie-Noëlle Anderson has always been a passionate champion of African causes. Her blood links with Africa have led her along an unusual and possibly unique path for a white woman and become a traditional healer. Marie-Noëlle Anderson has become, to all intents and purposes, a Ndebele. She has been completely accepted by this Zimbabwean community, absorbing its plant-related medicinal lore.

The serious threat posed by multinational pharmaceutical companies to the biodiversity of many African countries, and to plants with medicinal properties in particular, has driven Anderson to actively protect these resources through her commitment in various NGOs. Marie-Noëlle's endeavor is totally selfless since she works without monetary reward. Her efforts in drawing up an international document for the protection of endangered medicinal plants and for the preservation of the knowledge of traditional healers, as well as her commitment in ITHO and the Ndebele village, are a small but significant contribution to the protection of the biological and cultural heritage not only of Africa but of the entire planet.

to handle them. Sometimes all they do is make a small cut in the bark to extract sap, or take a small piece of root, or cut away a part. The 'wounded' tree can recover and be useful again. The healers respect the tree as a whole being, thus safeguarding its role in the environment.

Alas, pharmaceutical companies require large quantities of active principles, and after identifying them thanks to the healers, they proceed to plunder the forests. Only in a few cases have contracts been established between these companies and the local government. Even when this happens, the profits are rarely distributed to the local community. Once patents are granted, it becomes practically impossible to hold back exploitation of the resources. The damage becomes irreparable if we also take into account the socio-economic problems affecting many African countries. As has been the case in Zimbabwe, deforestation is frequently carried out by the poorest members of society, who indiscriminately cut down trees for firewood. Desertification advances and with it the inevitable loss of important tree species of crucial importance for traditional medicine. Some of those species are already seriously endangered.

Marie-Noëlle Anderson, who has an intimate knowledge of the situation in Africa and traditional medicine, serves as a link between the Décla-ration de Berne (and the WIPO) and the ITHO. She carries out research to trace already existing protocols in other countries, supplies information on the local situation, reports to members of the ITHO on the progress of work on the document, checks with them any modifications or updates to be made and refers this information back to the Déclaration de Berne. It is ceaseless, indispensable liaison work to exchange ideas. Anderson is also responsible for presenting the document to the ITHO and other associations of African healers, for example ZINATHA, the Zimbabwe National Traditional Healers Association, to check that it meets their requirements and safeguards biodiversity in their countries.

## The traditional Ndebele village

Marie-Noëlle Anderson's commitment to Africa, and the protection and promotion of the Ndebele people's culture, has also led to the creation of the Cecil John Rhodes Traditional Ndebele Village, situated in the district of Matobo, south of Bulawayo. The project was suggested by the wishes of the local Ndebele people and inspired by David Ngwenya. It aims to protect local traditions in agriculture, livestock breeding, medicine, crafts and building techniques and to preserve a culture which risks obliteration by unfettered modernization. The Ndebele are a proud warrior race and want to protect their age-old culture not by returning to the past but instead by ensuring that their knowledge is transmitted to future generations: for example, by teaching traditional crafts, traditional plant medicine and agriculture. These are the objectives of the project, which also brings a promise of self-sufficiency through income from responsible tourism, in the form of stays, visits, workshops and courses, and by the sale of locally produced arts and crafts.

So far the project has been officially recognized by the government but it is proving difficult to secure the funding necessary to complete the project.

The involvement of the ITHO in the village project is crucial, since it will be one of the centers for the protection and preservation of medicinal plants and the knowledge of traditional healers. It will be possible to take courses in traditional medicine onsite and local healers will work alongside doctors trained in Western medicine.

The vegetables that form the staple diet of the Ndebele, maize, millet, rapoko (a cereal with a small black grain, used to make flour and beer), peanuts (peanut paste is very popular), sweet potato and edible greens such as beet and spinach, will be grown in the village and cattle, goats and hens will also be raised.

*Alessandra Abbona*

# From the stories, the Presidia

*Paolo Di Croce*

How close can we get to the world? Just how can we see this huge, round planet from close up? And how can we hug it, protect it, console it and help it to rest? It would take thousands of hands, eyes and hearts. Thousands of feet would have to walk thousands of miles.

Slow Food has found another way: the Award jury. The hands, eyes, heart and feet of the Slow Food Movement are all there. It speaks all the languages of the world and, above all, listens to the world when it speaks. There are around 600 jurors for the Award and their number continues to grow. We would like to have a round thousand in 2004 and it looks as though we are going to reach that goal. Today, the jurors live in 80 different nations. Their activities and interests cross each other at every longitude and latitude. That's why one of the Peruvian winners in 2001 was nominated by a Dutch juror, and a Danish juror nominated an Australian.

There were 14 winners in 2001 and 13 in 2000 but the world has told us many more tales over the past two years. Meetings of the Award Presidency Committee, where nominees are chosen, are always lively since it gets more difficult every year to make the selections. Thanks to the jurors, hundreds of candidatures come in; hundreds of wonderful, true stories.

At times, they do not make it all the way to the award because while preserving some kind of biodiversity, they are either not strictly connected to the food world or are situations, that are in some way parallel. For example, the ones that concern biological farming methods are worthy of merit but do not risk extinction, or are not indigenous to the territory in question. This was the case with a beekeeper in Kamchatka, an organic farmer in California, and a researcher studying whales in Argentina.

On the other hand, it may just be that a choice has to be made. The award has a budget, a specific sum of money that must be used to the best advantage. This is where Presidency Committee meetings become

China. Photos Hiroiji Kubota, Magnum

stressful. Choices have to be made and sometimes it is not that easy. But those who miss out on an award have still won in a way. They have entered the world of Slow Food, a world that is a publishing house, an international movement and a Presidia office rolled into one.

Most of our readers already know what the Presidia are, at least in the Italian version. Presidia are either working projects that safeguard and protect products that have already boarded the Ark, or larger projects for cataloguing quality food products, whether animal, plant, culinary or manufactured. If any of the products looks as if it can be revived or sustained, then Slow Food, with the help of local groups and farms, attempts to give technical support, along with training, promotion or marketing, to help the producers protect the product. In Italy, more than a hundred Presidia have been started. They are small but effective sources of income and identity, small fortresses that protect productive, ecological and agricultural systems that must not disappear.

**From the Andes to the desert**

Naturally, exporting this model to the situations encountered in other continents or developing countries may not be easy. But reading the stories narrated in the candidatures convinced us that, simple or not, this was the path to take.

In the Argentinean Andes, a woman decided to revitalize potato production. Until 50 years ago, there were innumerable varieties of potatoes in this area, all very much part of a gastronomic culture that used them in a thousand different dishes and knew which ones to cultivate in different soil and climate situations. The woman began by organizing fairs so producers could meet and exchange seeds. She continued by working with farmers on quantity and distribution. She managed to get these potatoes from the Andes into supermarkets in Buenos Aires. But then two problems arose. First of all, people no longer knew how to use the potatoes so they bought them, cooked them badly, didn't enjoy them and never bought them again. Then came the problem of the crop health. Could the potatoes be defended with organic systems that would protect it from parasites without altering its wholesome quality? So is this not a Presidium? Is this not already almost a Presidium that, with the support of Slow Food, could find the help it needs, such as printing informative material for the consumer and expert consultation on organic agriculture to eliminate parasites?

In one of the most arid and desolate areas of Mexico, a 'philosopher with a talent for agriculture' managed to revive the production of amaranth, an ancient foodstuff with extraordinary nutritional properties

*Mongolia. Photos Hiroiji Kubota, Magnum*

and sensory characteristics. He worked alongside farmers, guaranteeing them a profit and helping stop the depopulation of an entire rural area to the advantage of the large cities, where farmers usually move to end up living in squalor. He has already done a lot, and he has rightly already received many awards, but there is a lot still left to do. In particular, he needs visibility and here is where Slow Food can be useful. This is where a Presidium can help.

There are dozens of stories like these. We tell them in our publications and on our website (www.slowfood.com). The Award always begins with the candidatures since those excluded one year are reconsidered the next. But we also tell these stories because this databank, this legacy of knowledge and skills, gives rise to many of our articles, many of our projects and many of our, and our collaborators', dreams.

The Slow Food Award for the Defense of Biodiversity was celebrated in Bologna in 2000 and Oporto in 2001. It will be celebrated again in Turin on 23 October 23, 2002, just before the Hall of Taste opens. The Award is one of the sources of life and energy for our movement because a greater and greater part of our work and commitment revolves around the defense of biodiversity. This Award is the public expression of a much broader and more complex task. The winners themselves become spokesmen for the Movement. There is even going to be a Slow Food Award Winners Club, a spontaneous group that will be involved in biodiversity worldwide. Along with all of us and, we are certain, all of you.

*Mongolia. Photo Hiroiji Kubota, Magnum*

*Huangshan, China. Photos Hiroiji Kubota, Magnum*

# The Chuyma Aru association

**T**he Chuyma Aru association was created in 1988 and officially recognized as an NGO in 1990. Since then, it has implemented small projects in co-operation with European and US NGOs. It was founded by agronomists Nestor and Walter Chambi, and a veterinary surgeon, Victor Quiso Choque. All three belong to the Aymara people. University education enabled them to get to know at close quarters what they now call 'the world of agronomists'. They consider it a very different, in too many respects hostile, world than that of the Aymaras. After several years working in the agronomists' universe, they decided to return to their roots and those of the Aymara culture, which they had been actively helping to erode.

**America, Peru, Puno**

**Desarrollismo and rural culture**
Nestor and Walter Chambi Pacoricona are brothers. After graduating in the early 1980s, they began working with the agencies of the Ministry of Agriculture, whose activities are noted for what is know in South America as their desarrollista tendencies. Desarrollo, or 'development', is the magic word that inspires projects implemented for the benefit of rural communities. But as the years passed, the Chambi brothers realized that the institutional programs set up to help the Aymara community were to a large extent failures. As soon as a project was completed and the agency withdrew, the community returned to its previous situation. Hardships were not

*Nestor and Walter Chambi*

relieved and there was no real transfer of knowledge. And every failure meant millions of dollars wasted. According to agronomists and professionals in general, it was always the fault of the peasant families: they didn't understand, they didn't do what they were supposed to, they didn't trust new methods. Initiative after initiative, project after project, doubts grew in the minds of Chambi and some of their colleagues. The development envisaged by government institutions was based on models that were too distant from the Aymara culture. Quantitative, mechanistic models regularly proved to be inappropriate for the Aymaran situation. "The first major misunderstanding came with the large-scale agrarian reforms of 1969," explains Nestor Chambi. "Land was given to the peasants, true, but it was divided into huge blocs to be transformed into agribusinesses that would produce for the market. But the market tends to standardize, while protection of biodiversity lies with diversification".

Here are a few examples. About 20 years ago there was a temporary climatic variation on the altiplano, the Andean highlands. The seasons were very regular and uniform for several years, without excessive rains or droughts. At precisely that moment, the Ministry of Agriculture started to recommend the seeds of 'improved' potatoes to peasants. At the time, the first harvests with the new potatoes were excellent. The tubers were large, some weighing up to one or two kilos, and harvests were plentiful. But then the ab-

normal climate pattern changed. Normal conditions returned, with droughts, floods, frosts and parasites. The new seeds proved to be delicate, deteriorating rapidly and succumbing to frost. It was necessary to return to the old varieties, which were better suited to the altiplano climate. However, since the arrival of the new potatoes, people had no longer been storing the seeds of the old varieties. A huge number of potato varieties disappeared as a result. Where the institutions had worked hardest, losses were greatest. "Government bodies," Chuyma Aru managers point out, "have to work for the market and therefore tend to standardize but in the Andes, it is normal to sow many varieties of potato in the same field, sometimes 200 different types. In this way, frost, floods or drought can only damage part of the crop". Irrigation channels are another problem. In traditional Andean agriculture, they are dug directly into the soil. When the government got involved, channels began to be lined with concrete. Soil channels permit a certain amount of water to seep out, giving rise to the spontaneous growth of grass and weeds along the edges, which serve as free forage for animals and have deep roots which act like sponges in the soil, absorbing water from aquifers. This allows the soil to maintain a certain level of moisture deep down, even if it appears to be dry on the surface. When concrete is used, seepage along the path of the channel is prevented – a waste of water, according to agronomists. All the earth round about dries out and cracks begin to form in the soil. The little moisture in the soil evaporates through these cracks and drought intensifies. The upshot is that the new concrete channels are almost always abandoned after a short time and the peasant families return to their traditional channels dug in the earth. Agronomists have established that a water flow of one liter per second is needed per hectare of land. But the knowhow of the Andean people has demonstrated that a channel with a flow of six liters per second can irrigate over 100 hectares. That's the difference between a soil channel and a concrete channel.

## The Aymara and betrayal at school

To understand, we will have to change our terminology. The key word is not development but crianza. This is the word used to indicate the cultivation of the land, the breeding of livestock and the raising of children. But the verb criar means more than that. It means taking care of something and establishing a mutual relationship. It is not a one-sided activity. In the Andean world, everyone and everything are criadores. Not just men, women and children but also all other things, the weather, the climate, the seasons and the stars. Everyone and everything gives and receives; everyone and everything has a meaning and offers respect.

Everything is interconnected; every being has a culture, language and function. The productive unit for Andean culture is never one man or one woman but a couple: life only exists in the

whole. For an Andean family, the earth is a daughter when it is fed before sowing, a bride when it is sown, a sister when it begins to produce, and a mother when it offers its fruit to its children. The pachamama, the word used to describe the earth in the Quechua language, is respected and loved; it is a living being. A farmer cannot decide how to treat the earth without first consulting all the other elements involved, first and foremost the earth itself. But there are also all the other things involved in producing a crop: the rain, the moon, animals and signs. An agronomist may look at his calendar and decide to sow in a week's time because by so doing, he will be able to harvest and sell the crop at a certain date. The Aymara have to 'talk' to the earth to see if it wants to be sown, with the moon to see if it is in the right phase, with the rain and because if it hasn't rained you cannot sow. On the basis of all these signs, they decide what to sow. For the years are not all the same. Some are rainy and suitable for potatoes while others are dry and good for corn.

The Aymara look at the world from close up. They penetrate the subtle patterns that combine to form nature and, with the unhurried gentleness of the old people, and the enthusiasm and adaptability of children, each day confirm their participation as equals in the complex system of existence.

Andeans do not plan because the world is a living being, not something that can be arranged and rearranged at will. "The earth," they say, "is not a

legacy from our ancestors but a loan from our children".

Where did the break occur? Where do the traces of an age-old culture fade away? At school. From the age of six to 20, children and young people are progressively alienated from their roots. At school and university, students increasingly become part of a different world. A world in which, for example, there are four seasons: spring, summer, autumn and winter. In Peru, however, there are only two: one cold and dry and the other wet and warmer. Of the eleven climate types to be found in the world, eight exist somewhere in Peru while further north, the climate is less varied. Temperatures can vary by 20 degrees from morning to evening and the soil of cultivable land is never more the 25 centimeters deep so the machinery used in the northern hemisphere is ineffectual. At school, children study a world which is not the one around them and has nothing in common with Andean culture.

### Relearning

Chuyma Aru, which means 'the heart of the Aymara', was founded with two main objectives, as a result of the above considerations. The first, of a theoretical and educational nature, is called 're-ethnification' and is directed at people who have left the community to study. It is a way of relearning how to live in a rural community. The most important part of this reconciliation is the ritual element that focuses on the Andean world-view, enables participants to understand its development and mechanisms.

**Motives for Slow Food Award**

Chuyma Aru refuses to compromise. The association is part of a broader movement of thought and action which has as its main objectives the conservation and recovery of ancient agricultural techniques. It is 20 years since Pratec, the Proyecto Andino de Tecnologías Campesinas, or 'Andean Project for Peasant Technologies' was founded. Today, Chuyma Aru is one of the 18 core units of the project with specific responsibility for training. The aim is to recover the past in its purest form. As often happens with extreme positions, there is a risk of becoming detached from reality. The peasants have to cope with everyday life, and often associations seeking to defend their culture aim at a pureness of principle that is impractical for the farmers. However, the decade-long efforts of Chuyma Aru has been of crucial importance for the recovery of endangered plant and animal varieties, for re-establishing contacts among the various communities in the Titicaca area, for creating a new professional awareness among agronomists and veterinarians, and even for slowly but surely bringing educational institutions closer to the local agricultural situation. The Slow Food Award is an acknowledgement of the value of the work carried out so far by this small NGO. It is a valuable opportunity for the project managers to compare their activities with those of other defenders of biodiversity in the international community. All, in their different ways, are working to protect the world so dear to the Aymara.

Chuyma Aru's projects in this area mainly consist of seminars and meetings between communities. The seminars are held at various localities in the vast area that centers on Puno (Conima, Mo, Tilali and so on). They generally last a week and deal with various topics providing opportunities for families to talk and compare their lives, their methods and their memories. The technical advisors coordinate and learn at the same time. Twice a year, an interregional journey round Lake Titicaca and beyond is organized to facilitate the circulation of solutions that the various communities have adopted. The journeys last about ten days and are both tiring and expensive, especially in terms of the time which the farmers have to take away from their farming and families. Yet they are also essential for the Chuyma Aru project. When the farmers return to their communities, they have new stimuli and ideas, an input that comes from their own people, who share their needs and their respect for the world.

The second area of activity is more practical and is aimed at strengthening the culture of the various crianzas to be nurtured: plants, animals, the sky, air, water, rituals and so on. There are five intervention routes for this second area: plants and the 'seed path' around Lake Titicaca and beyond; Andean animals; the countryside; craft activities and the storage of agricultural products, from textiles to food, hats and pottery; and organic agriculture. Some important results have already been achieved. A census of potatoes, for example, and the re-activa-

tion of the 'seed path' with the farmers' journeys and the bartering of seed, have already led to a noticeable increase in the number of potato varieties farmed by families in the area. The number, formerly about 200 varieties per family, had seriously declined, dropping to fewer than ten. Now it has settled at around 30-40 varieties per family, thanks to the resumption of exchanges between different communities.

Organic agriculture was also seriously endangered and had to be revived. In the 1960s and 1970s, technical experts convinced 96 percent of Andean peasant farmers to make extensive use of chemical fertilizers and pesticides, thus damaging the land and contributing to an increase in, and spread of, disease. When they decided to stop, the land had been so badly depleted that even worms were rare, the very worms the Aymara call the 'cooks of the plants' because they process the minerals in the soil for them.

"Today the situation has changed," says Nestor Chambi, "The people who still persist in using chemicals and fertilizers are large companies, the owners of land who do not live on it but in the city. Or they are agronomists".

The managers of Chuyma Aru are at pains to explain that their activity in the rural communities is accompanying and not consultancy. What they have embarked upon is a shared journey, an ongoing exchange between community and technical advisors. In the end, it's all a matter of crianza.

*C. S.*

# The poppy growers of Ismailkoy

**A**fyon, capital of the province of the same name on the western Anatolian plateau in Turkey, is a city of about 100,000 residents. It acts as a showcase for the food products of the vast farming area round about, including sausages, cakes and sweets, cheese, honey, milk and meat. Until 30 years ago, there were over 20 presses in Afyon that made poppy seed oil. Today, there are only three, and to survive they have to rely on income from the sale of sunflower seed oil. It is not a question of market forces, either. Even though sunflower seed oil costs around USD 0.65 per liter against USD 1.10 for poppy seed oil, consumers prefer poppy seed oil. There is simply not enough of it.

**Europe, Turkey, Anatolia, Ismailkoy**

**Opium, oil and prohibition**

Afyon, the city's name, means 'opium' in Turkish. There is evidence that opium poppies, *Papaver somnifer anatolicum*, have been grown in Turkey for at least 1,000 years, and the place-name is confirmation of the historic link between local agriculture and the plant. The part of the flower that contains opium is not the seed but the rind of the large capsule containing the seeds. Extraction of the resin, which is then for smoking or conversion into morphine, and then heroin, has to be carried out manually by making slight incisions on the capsule immediately after flowering. But for the people of this area, the poppy is important for its seeds, which have always been used as a food and in cooking. The seeds have a very high oil content and can be processed for use in many different ways. They can be toasted or ground and sprinkled on bread and other bakery products. Alternatively, a very full-flavored oil can be extracted from them to provide one of the staple ingredients of Anatolian cooking. The toasted seeds are used to flavor bread. Ground coarsely, they turn into an oily flour that is added to the dough for pastries and biscuits. Further grinding produces a soft spread which used on bread, or as a coating for baked food. With added sugar, they make an energy-rich snack. It has an unmistakable flavor, somewhat reminiscent of peanut butter but with a stronger taste, part nutty and part grainy. Oil is obtained by slightly heating this mixture to facilitate extraction and pressing. It is used as a dressing or for frying. The very low melting point makes it ideal for the rapid baking methods used in the Turkish cuisine of the Anatolian plateau.

The crisis began in 1970, when the US administration under Richard Nixon decided that it was necessary to take firm action on the heroin problem. Although a CIA report indicated that much larger quantities of illegal opium were being produced in India, Afghanistan, Pakistan, Thailand, Laos and Burma than in Turkey, it was Turkey that was singled out for attention. This was essentially for two reasons. First, drug traffic from Turkey to Beirut or Marseilles was, although less significant than that on the other routes, the only one that the CIA's Bureau of Narcotics and Dangerous Drugs had investigated fully. The second, more important, reason was that Turkey was a member of NATO and depended on US military assistance. The fact was that with Turkey, the US could exert its authority. At that time, with the war in Vietnam claiming victims among the very young men whom Nixon thought it imperative to save from heroin, there was a need to mount an operation quickly and successfully. At the end negotiations in 1972, six areas in Turkey were identified where the cultivation of opium poppies could continue under strict controls. One of these areas was Afyon. But production was cut back drastically and subject to complicated licensing procedures.

## The best kaymak of all

Ismailkoy is a village of 600 inhabitants a few kilometers from Afyon. It has always been a poppy-growing village and even today, is the one which is most determined to keep it, refusing to switch to crops, such as sugar beet and vegetables in general. Each year, the Turkish authorities decide the extent and location of the areas for poppy cultivation. The cultivation zones and farmers involved change every year. Poppies are a crop that requires little attention or expense, and there is little risk. The

*Recep Koç*

seeds are planted in September and the plants flower from April to May with little irrigation and no treatment. Poppies are hardy, surviving Anatolia's hot dry climate well, even if the yield of oil from seeds is reduced in years of drought. The only activity required of the farmers, apart from watering and fertilizing the ground, is to thin them out when the flowers grow too thickly. The poppy plant, which reaches a height of 120 to 130 centimeters, is left to dry and then cut. The stalk is used as a cooking fuel, the capsules containing the seeds are sold to a pharmaceutical company, and the seeds are used as food. The people of Ismailkoy do not wish to lose a flavor which has been part of their and their ancestors' lives. This spirited resistance has deep, and unexpected, roots.

Afyon is famous not only for poppies, but also for kaymak. This is a cream prepared from milk that takes the form of very white, firm disks about one centimeter thick. It is eaten fresh, one or two days after it is made, to fully appreciate the flavor of the milk; it is hard enough to cut with a knife but at the same time extraordinarily creamy. The best kaymak comes from buffalo milk, with cow's milk following. It is made all over Turkey to be eaten with cakes and sweets or fruit in syrup. Otherwise, it can be spread on bread with a little honey. But the kaymak from the Afyon area is universally acknowledged to be the finest there is. The farmers of Ismailkoy are not only poppy growers. They have also always been livestock farmers. Each holding will only have a few head of buffalo or cattle but production is steady. And every day they go to the market at Afyon to sell their best kaymak, the part that will command the best prices.

What does kaymak have to do with poppies? When poppy seeds are pressed to obtain oil, the solid residue in the sacks of jute or nylon used to sieve the seed mixture is dried and stored. It comes in rectangular blocks called küspe, weighing about seven kilograms. These are crumbled into water as feed for buffalo, cows, goats and chickens. It is highly nutritious, rich in protein, fats and sugars. Each küspe costs about one dollar and provides up to four meals for a buffalo, one day's food. It is expensive but a buffalo can produce up to 12 liters of milk a day, yielding six portions of kaymak that sell for about a dollar and a half each. They have no doubts, "If our kaymak is the best, it is only thanks to the poppies. That is the only difference between the feed for our animals and what all the other animals in Turkey eat. Our animals' meat is better, too". The people of Ismailkoy can distinguish the flavor of the milk produced by poppy seed oil-fed animals from other milk. And they prefer it to other milk.

### The price of regulation

At Bolvadin, 40 kilometers from Ismailkoy, there is a factory that makes alkaloids, specifically morphine for pharmaceutical companies. Significantly, it belongs to the Ministry of Agriculture, and not to the Ministry of Health, as might seem logical. The factory was opened in 1980 with the aim of reversing the trend of progressively less land being used in this area to grow poppies. The Turkish government decided to support poppy production and since it could not openly defy the US by demanding an increase in production, it decided to take this alternative route. But its intention was to protect the traditional economic activities of the area.

Poppies are left to dry in the ground and once the capsules have dried, they are split open to remove the seeds and sold to the factory for about USD 0.70 per kilogram. The 2001 harvest yielded a total of 130 tons of dry capsules, and about the same quantity of seeds. The farmers keep part of the seeds for their own personal consumption, part of it is sold for oil pressing, at about USD 0.45 per kilogram, and they have part pressed to yield oil for their own consumption. The dark gray-black seeds from blue poppies contain less oil than the yellow or brown seeds from yellow, white or red poppies and are sold to companies that make coloring agents. In this way, the farmers whose land has been approved for cultivation earn considerable revenue between July and August from the sale of their crop. This money will be used to cover their fixed costs over the whole year, and perhaps for the following year if their land is selected for poppy cultivation, while the sale of kaymak and other agricultural products will go towards covering their other expenses. Today, the farmers of Ismailkoy are aware that they cannot ask their government to exert pressure on the US to increase the area under cultivation. Nevertheless, they hope that the Ministry of Agriculture will permit the factory to expand processing capacity in view of the steady demand for morphine from pharmaceutical companies.

What we have described is a sound economy, based on a mechanism of exchange and use: poppies, food, animal feed, animals and kaymak. There is no emigration from the village of Ismailkoy and young people are happy to carry on their families' activities. Yet this sound economy is not a secure one. Each year, everything is discussed anew; each year there may be a new regulation to comply with. The mountain and red tape that the poppy growers have to deal with is so daunting that many farmers in neighboring villages have given up. This has not happened at Ismailkoy, thanks to Recep Koç, the mayor, who takes care of all the bureaucratic formalities for the growers. Each year before sowing, a survey of every poppy-growing plot has to be carried out, specifying the surface area and estimating the crop yield. These forms are signed and sent to the authorities, who may visit to make checks during the year and see if the areas indicated on paper actually correspond to the land under cultivation. If there is a frost or an unexpected calamity that ruins the crop in a field, there is more paper, more inspections and more reports to justify the discrepancy between the estimate and the actual crop. The growers are closely supervised and even the delivery of dry capsules to the pharmaceutical plant is itself a precautionary measure. As we said, traditional opium extraction can only be carried out immediately after flowering by cutting the capsule. If the capsule not cut and left to dry, the active ingredient has to be extracted with a chemical process that cannot readily be replicated in the home.

The growers of Ismailkoy have accepted the rules and grow poppies in accordance with the agreed compromise. They are concerned about losing poppy seeds, an important part of their economy and culture, and the government is worried that poppy production might fuel the illegal trade in opium, morphine and heroin.

The people in the village have already abandoned many of their traditions. They no longer make infusions of poppy petals to soothe coughs. Only a few still collect the leaves from the first shoots to make salad. And nobody makes incisions in the capsules just after flowering to obtain a little opium resin to use as a medicine, particularly for children. It is as though the flowers in the wonderful spring fields were a threat rather than a resource. Any irregular behavior runs the risk of incurring heavy sanctions, if not imprisonment.

The fall in poppy production has led to other losses. Oil is no longer produced in Ismailkoy. Three presses operated before the restrictions were introduced. Now the people would like to reopen at least one so they are not forced to go to Afyon to buy oil and küspe for their livestock. Occupations have also disappeared in the rest of the country. When there used to be a large number of presses in Afyon, the solid that was deposited on the bottom of the oil containers was sent to Bodrum to make an excellent soap. Now the quantities available are so small that they no longer justify production and only the occasional vet still uses the residue to treat wounds or skin diseases in animals.

*C. S.*

---

**Motives for Slow Food Award**

Recep Koç and his fellow villagers have conducted, and partially won, an unequal battle. What supports the economy of Ismailkoy is a delicate balance of many interrelated activities that involves the whole village, from the men who work the land and the women who make bread, to the few remaining oil-pressers in Afyon to the farmers whose animals produce kaymak. This fragile equilibrium has had to face a giant like the US. Unable to intervene effectively against the illegal production of opium in the Far East, the United States could only exert heavy-handed pressure on Turkey over its limited illicit traffic to France and Lebanon.

The farmers in Ismailkoy have managed to keep going so far but the community needs a local economy with better defined prospects. The growers need to be able to plan better for the future, and the prospect of something other than a mountain of red tape. The Slow Food Award will enable them to achieve greater visibility and will help the world to think about this part of the planet, which has been growing poppies for more than a millennium.

# Thierno Maadjou Bah Mamadou Mouctar Sow

**T**hierno Maadjou Bah, born in 1944, and Mamadou Mouctar Sow, born in 1952, are both originally from the Futah Djallon region, which sprawls across Mali and Guinea. They belong to the Peulh ethnic group and come from farming families of average means who own vegetable plots, banana plantations, or small arable or livestock farms.

During early childhood, they witnessed the exploitation of colonial administration, which forced their parents to give the state all their harvested crops (rubber, néré, pepper) and animal produce (milk, eggs, livestock and so on). They were profoundly affected by that difficult period, and their family upbringing made them aware of their socio-economic and cultural environment, so they quickly recognized the vital importance of the néré tree (*Parkia biglobosa*), which has pharmacological properties and numerous applications as a food. Many parts of the tree are used, from roots to leaves, bark, flowers and seeds, from which a traditional seasoning ingredient called soumbara is obtained.

With the hope of one day being able to help improve the rural population's difficult living conditions, the two finished their studies, Thierno in agricultural economics and Mamadou in agriculture.  They re-

**mained aware of the importance of conservation and became the main coordinators of an action plan to protect the néré tree, a symbol of biodiversity and key to survival for the peoples of Futah Djallon.**

## Africa, Guinea, Futah Djallon

**Thierno Maadjou Bah** won a scholarship to study journalism in the German Democratic Republic after graduating in Conakry. He specialized in economics and also undertook a work experience program at Radio Berlin International.

After returning to Guinea in 1973, Thierno Maadjou was taken on as a staff writer at the Ministry of Information but to escape the repressive regime, he asked to be transferred to the Ministry of Rural Development at Labé.

This was finally an opportunity to get involved in agriculture and communication in a rural area. The economist became a farmer and set up, amongst other things, composting projects that relieved the town of Labé of organic waste disposal problems. In addition, he organized a scheme to spread cultivation of potatoes, maize, beans and manioc without chemical fertilizers or pesticides, which resulted in increased yields.

In 1990, Thierno Maadjou was ap-pointed manager of the radio station Radio Rurale de la Moyenne Guinée and inspired the first broadcasts on how to farm using modern methods, at the same time educating listeners about conservation and fire prevention on the savanna. He also energetically campaigned against the use of néré wood as a fuel for brick ovens.

**Mamadou Mouctar Sow** studied agronomy at the University of Conakry after completing his high school diploma in agriculture and animal husbandry. From 1975 al 1979, he continued his studies at the University of Santa Clara in Cuba, where he graduated in livestock engineering.

After returning to Guinea he worked at the Bureau d'Etudes du Ministère de la Pêche et de l'Elevage (Research Center of the Ministry of Fisheries and Animal Husbandry), studying feed for ruminant animals. He then moved to the Ferme Agricole de Kolaboui

*Thierno Maadjou Bah*

(Kolaboui Agricultural Farm) at Boké, where he had worked on problems concerning the nutrition of poultry and pigs, and improving the protein level of animal feed in general. He experimented with various locally available products, including the yellow néré powder. He is a researcher in the field of animal nutrition, a member of the Comité National Ramsar for the protection of endangered species and carries out, working with farmers, experiments to safeguard plants used as fodder and the néré tree.

## The néré tree

*Parkia biglobosa* is a tree that can reach 20 meters in height, grows in sandy soils, has an umbrella-shaped crown, and a long, flat, slightly curved fruit pod. The tree is now threatened by indiscriminate felling for firewood, or deforestation by farmers seeking land for planting.

The néré tree has outstanding food value as well as pharmacological properties. The flesh of the fruit is rich in carbohydrates (80 percent), minerals (calcium, phosphorus) and vitamins (A and C). Its seeds – rich in protein, fats and carbohydrates – are used as a condiment or seasoning. In the past, they were used as a substitute for coffee. Various parts of the tree, well-known for its properties as a diuretic, laxative and vermifuge, are used to treat illnesses such as dysentery, intestinal parasitosis, bronchitis, asthma, ulcers, rickets, toothache, sore throat and dermatitis. It can also be used as a dye. The dried seeds are used as fodder for animals. When boiled, fermented and ground to a paste, called soumbara, they constitute the basic seasoning ingredient for the local cuisine. Their fundamental role in nutrition derives from their high content of protein, vitamins of the B group, minerals and trace elements. Finally, the tree also improves the quality of the soil.

## Soumbara versus Maggi stock cubes

Soumbara, the néré seasoning, is made by first fermenting and then roasting, grinding and sieving the tree's seeds. The resulting paste is kneaded and divided into small balls. It is nutritious, with a high protein and energy content.

Guinea is the third poorest country in the world, despite having abundant agricultural and food resources. Biodiversity in the area is still almost intact and the people have a natural tendency to preserve their traditions. Unfortunately, poverty and the struggle for survival, on top of economic pressure from foreign multinationals, are causing some traditional locally grown food produce to disappear. This is further impoverishing the farming community whose

*Mamadou Mouctar Sow*

existence is inseparably linked to these products.

In particular, Nestlé, the producer of Maggi stock cubes, is causing significant problems. Maggi cubes have swamped the market all over Guinea. They are sold very cheaply and are available everywhere so the consumption of soumbara has dropped dramatically. But people do not choose Maggi cubes because of the price. Although very cheap, it is not competitive with the traditional seasoning ingredient, but other social and cultural factors come into play.

To promote Maggi stock cubes, Nestlé has adopted various strategies supported by massive advertising. Every day, radio, local television and newspapers carry commercials translated into the three national languages. At weekly markets, girls with bullhorns shout slogans advertising Maggi cubes, handing out T-shirts and tote bags to ram home the message. The best salesgirls can even win a trip to Mecca. Nestlé also makes modest donations towards the building of schools, health clinics and mosques. Opinion polls have recently been carried out among the population. Although consumption of Maggi cubes has increased – there are cubes for every taste – at the expense of soumbara, even for making traditional rice-based dishes like lafidi or foutti. In other cases, rural residents continue to use both soumbara and other, more natural and cheaper, traditional ingredients. As a rule, however, it seems to be old people who use it. Soumbara is considered a food 'for poor people' whereas Maggi cubes are 'modern'.

Owing to Maggi monopoly, the economy of rural communities is changing. Women who used to collect néré fruit and make soumbara have had to start growing vegetables. But this earns much less money than soumbara used to when it was widely used in the community.

## Women at work

From the moment they first met, the two experts understood each other for both feel passionately about the same problems. One tradition of the Peulh people is for members of the same family to gather and discuss their plans for farming. It was during one of these family meetings that Bah and Sow met and while looking round the fields, they discovered that all the biggest trees, including néré trees, had been cut down, even though the including néré trees were protected in their village. They began to think about this problem and also talked about it on the radio in agriculture and ecology broadcasts. In 1996, the two set up a reforestation program to protect trees that were valuable for humans, such as the néré, and for animals, such as fig trees. Figs produce a very small fruit in Guinea because of the lack of water. Their fruit is dried, ground and then mixed with other animal fodder. More than 3,000 trees growing in fields of the cereal crop fonio, (*Digitaria exilis*), have been saved and protected in the last five years. The project covers an area of about 10 hectares in the district of Ley Miro, in the prefecture of Pita. A further 100 hectares in the same region has been declared a protected area.

Thierno and Mamadou have also founded an NGO, the Association des Jeunes Volontaires pour le Développement de Timbi (Association of Young Volunteers for the Development of Timbi). Timbi is the flat zone in the region of Futah Djallon, where a tree nursery with 20,000 saplings has been set up. At the same time, the two have carried out education and information programs on soumbara. Over the past two years, they have met women's organizations interested in processing neré seeds into soumbara and selling it. Thanks to this program of information and education, soumbara production has recovered and as many as seven groups of women are once more involved in this traditional occupation. In the year 2000, they put seven tons of neré seeds onto the market, some of it already processed to soumbara.

*Claire Panzer*

**Motives for Slow Food Award**

In isolation and without resources, Mamadou and Thierno have created a project that protects and recovers a basic feature of the culture, traditions and economy of the third-poorest country in the world, in competition with a model of multinational capitalism like Nestlé.

The Slow Food Award will help the two to emerge from the isolation in which they have worked so far, enabling them to further develop their project.

*Special Jury Award*

# Pablo Jara

**P**ablo Rafael Jara Valdivia was born in Santiago, Chile in 1953. His family was well known in the construction industry and Pablo began to work for the company after finishing his mechanical engineering studies. In 1984, the year of the great change, he was a successful engineer with the family firm, married and father of a one-year old baby girl. Pablo was then just over 30, at least 20 kilograms overweight, and suffering from a range of allergies which considerably restricted his outdoor life. He also had serious digestive problems. He was unhappy, weighed down by his physical ailments and a slave to antihistamines and their side effects. His life changed thanks to a friend who listened to his complaints and simply advised, "Eat a bit better and you'll soon feel better". He recommended a macrobiotic restaurant in the center of Santiago and Jara was practically adopted by the chefs there.

**America, Chile, Santiago**

**The discovery of quinoa**
Until then, food and eating had been of little importance to Jara. Following his friend's advice, he focused his attention first on whole-grain rice, which was the healthiest food he was aware of, and which he ate every day at his new restaurant. The first improvements were soon evident: he digested his food properly and lost weight. But attention to what he

was eating, and the effects that food had on his body, soon developed into an interest in food itself as something with its own history and identity. He quickly realized that whole-grain rice had very little to do with South American or Andean identity. Research into the staple foods of the Mapuche, the original inhabitants of Chile, soon led him to discover quinoa. More than 15 years have passed since that time and Pablo Jara does more than just eat quinoa almost every day, or bring up his daughter on quinoa. He has traveled all over Chile and other Andean countries, seeking information and instruction. He has interviewed farmers, particularly the older ones, to find out why, when and to what extent the custom of eating quinoa had disappeared in Chile. He formulated theories, tested them, disproved them, constructed better ones and so on. He tried to grow quinoa, with admittedly limited success, but more significantly, he persuaded a number of farmers from the coastal area and central provinces of Chile to sow quinoa, recovering their skills and the skills of their forefathers. He then bought the crop, cleaned it, sold it to packing companies and exported it. Now, 16 years on from his first encounter with quinoa, Pablo Jara is able to advise and assist farmers who have decided to grow this crop. Quinoa is sold in shops and macrobiotic restaurants, as well as some supermarkets.

## Dehusking machines

There's a way of telling people who have just discovered quinoa from those who know it as a household food: listen to how they pronounce the word. The Mapuche still pronounce it 'quingwa', which, in the somewhat guttural pronunciation of their language, sounds something like 'kin-hua'. Others, of mixed race or people who have started eating quinoa recently, pronounce it according to the simpler Spanish transliteration, 'kìnoa'. There are many other names and ways of pronouncing the word – dague, quingoa, quinua, quingua – which shows how deeply it is rooted in the native culture.

Quinoa is a crop of the Andean highlands which was widely cultivated in Peru, Bolivia and the north of Chile in pre-Colombian times. The scientific name for the plant, which has a one-meter high stem and a plume-like flower, is *Chinopodium quinoa wild* and the edible part consists of the small, dried, seeds of the flower. During the harvest season, the plants are cut at the base and the flowers are laid out to dry. The stems and leaves are used as animal fodder. The seeds are then removed and have to be separated from the cuticle, since this contains bitter, tannic inedible saponin, and was once used as a detergent. The traditional way to remove the cuticle is by soaking the grains in water, causing them to swell and the outer coating to split. At this point, the cuticle is removed by repeated rinsing until it no longer makes foam. The grains are then dried again so that they can be stored. Another system is to toast the seeds. Once the grains have been toasted, the cuticle can easily be rubbed off.

These methods are still widely used but Pablo Jara in his search for healthy foods has gone even further, invoking the biodynamic philosophy of food. In his opinion quinoa, either toasted or dehusked in water and dried, is a dead food, devoid of vital energy. True, it provides calories and nutrients but it cannot germinate and no longer contains energy. Quinoa should be dehusked dry, like rice. Jara has made use of his skills as a mechanical engineer to come up with a solution, a sort of cross between a rice dehusking machine and one for dehusking corn, with a part he has specially invented to remove impurities.

Though dry dehusking machines actually do exist, Jara – typically – likes to do things the hard way, achieving goals that have long been reached elsewhere but have been forgotten in Chile. That's why he built his own quinoa machine, which is much more powerful than those on the market and much less expensive than one bought new.

## The powerful, the peasants and the intellectuals

Quinoa has been grown on the Andean plateau for thousands of years. In pre-Colombian times, it was a food reserved for the powerful. It is very rich in protein and energy, as well as being very digestible. There are various varieties of quinoa, suitable for different climates, different soils and different altitudes. Apparently, quinoa can be grown anywhere and is very adaptable but in fact there are many varieties. In the bigger producer nations, such as Bolivia, varieties with lighter seeds tend to be preferred. Indeed, quinoa is now popularly known as blanquita, or 'white stuff'. But just as quinoa flowers can have different colors, so too the seeds can be various shades of white, yellow, brown and gray. Incidentally, the whitest seeds are frequently the ones with the least flavor. Jara encourages 'his' farmers to grow seeds in a range of colors. When he collects the harvested grains for dehusking, and separates those to be used as seed, he mixes seeds from all his producers together to redistribute them and circulate them all around Chile. In the Inca empire, quinoa, like amaranth, was thought to be an aphrodisiac. Its highly nutritious powers were reserved for the élite. Quinoa was eaten by the political and religious establishment in a civilization where the very bases of power were bound up in food, its production, storage and distribution. The Spanish grasped that the crop was used by the Incas as a means of maintaining power in their kingdom and differentiating between the castes. They banned the cultivation of quinoa, replacing it with other crops, such as corn and wheat. Quinoa only continued to be grown in the remotest areas, which the Spaniards couldn't control. In those isolated, the roots of quinoa went deep. Here, even if it is only for self-consumption, quinoa is grown and has by no means disappeared from historical memory and the daily table. Obviously, it has become the food of mountaineers and peasants. City dwellers have no memory of quinoa and once something has been forgotten, it is hard to recover.

Chile has received a great deal of immigration from Europe. Only about 2,000,000 families are considered native Chilean, all the others having immigrated at various times. Until a few years ago, quinoa was thus associated with the poorest social groups. Then, in 1983, the annual FAO conference stressed the need to encourage the production and consumption of so-called minor crops, and native foods of vegetable origin. The 1980s were, in Chile as elsewhere, years of fast food as a symbol of progress. Hamburgers and fries were all the rage. The FAO recommendation was not entirely without effect, however, and some early movers were already active. Pablo Jara discovered quinoa at that time, in 1985. It was the year when he began to collect his first few kilograms from the farmers who had continued to grow it for self-consumption. Pablo now processes about 250 tons per year and has been exporting since 1991, mainly to the United States. Quinoa is already a familiar product in places like San Francisco, while, ironically, most people in Santiago still have no idea what it is.

But the recovery has started. Among the purchasers of quinoa you can, of course, find the children and grandchildren of those who have always eaten it but there are also people in search of food that is not only healthy, wholesome and natural, but also authentic, associated with tradition and native to a well-defined region. This is a result of the increased awareness brought about by better education, itself the consequence of higher living standards.

So in Chile, quinoa is once again a food for the upper classes, not because it is prohibitively expensive – quite the reverse – but because a class of university-educated people with a preference for a macrobiotic diet is rescuing this kind of foodstuff. Quinoa is already on sale in supermarkets that stock natural or health foods and gradually, memories and knowledge from the past are being reawakened. Pablo Jara watches this growth in consumption not so much with the pleasure of a businessman seeing his profits increase but rather with the satisfaction of a thinker seeing his ideas vindicated.

**In the kitchen**

There are many ways to cook with quinoa. Like rice, it can be used for soups, hot or cold dishes, as a vegetable side dish or eaten with salad, vegetables, meat or fish. It can even be served with fruit as a dessert. Once boiled, it will keep in the fridge for several days, up to two or three weeks. It is an age-old foodstuff that can adapt perfectly to the demands of modern cuisine. It does not require too much preparation – about 15-20 minutes – and provides light, healthy, easily digestible dishes. Quinoa contains no gluten so it cannot be made into bread on its own but quinoa flour can be mixed with wheat-flour to make wonderfully fragrant bread. Toasted quinoa flour has been used since ancient times to prepare chicha, the generic name for drinks obtained from sugared and fermented cereals, or it can be used to make sweets, or simply added to either hot or cold milk to aromatize it and make it more nutritious.

Santiago restaurants are tentatively beginning to serve quinoa as a side dish, like boiled rice. Jara is certain, however, that the imagination of good chefs, together with the expectations of a demanding, food-conscious public will soon do full justice to the versatility of this precious South American resource.

*C. S.*

### Motives for Slow Food Award

Chile has followed a path that in some respects runs parallel to those of other Latin American countries. It is a conservative country, which has somehow healed the wounds left by the years of dictatorship and can today point to economic stability it has painfully, but very clearly, achieved. In this restructuring process, the Andean soul has pushed increasingly away from the center of national consciousness and relegated to the status of a crystallized, and essentially sterile, museum piece. In this situation, where traditional culture is repressed, Pablo Jara's work has value from several viewpoints because the recovery of quinoa in Chile is significant in many ways.

It is a cultural recovery, which has rescued the knowledge of the older generation. It is a recovery of identity, since through quinoa, recognition has been given to the Mapuche ethnic group, which has undergone greater marginalization and progressive rejection in Chile than elsewhere. It is a recovery of production, since quinoa can yield excellent results on land unsuited for other crops.

And it is also an economic recovery, since the farmers involved by Jara can earn significant income.

As well as being a prestigious acknowledgement for the work Jara has stubbornly carried forward over the last 15 years at considerable economic sacrifice, the Slow Food Award will give Jara the visibility he lacks today and provide encouragement for the growers. It will help quinoa to start a new phase in its checkered career and transform itself from a delicacy for intellectual health freaks into a dish regularly served at the tables of lovers of good food all over the world.

# Rew Kuang Choon

**R**ew Kuang Choon was born 54 years ago on the island of Namhae, in the province of Kyongsang Nam in the extreme south of South Korea. Six years before he was born, his father bought a jukbang, one of the traditional island fishing enclosures, and from that moment on, the Rew family dedicated itself to anchovies.

Little Kuang Choon joined his father immediately after graduating from junior high school and his wife Hee Re Park, now 47.

## Asia, South Korea, Jijuk-ri, Namhae Kun

### The island of anchovies

Korea is a peninsula girt by three seas and fishing has always made a major contribution to the national economy. Korean cuisine has an abundance of fish dishes and anchovies are one of the most sought-after delicacies. In the year 2000, 201,000 tons of anchovies were caught by Korean fishermen and only 1,000 tons went for export.

Namhae, with an area of 356 km$^2$, is third largest of South Korea's 3,000 islands. Located in the northern part of the Hallyo Marine Park, it is an area where anchovies are a source of pride since, with garlic, they are Namhae's most celebrated local product. Garlic is rotated with rice in the local fields and the island looks very different according to the time of year and the crop being grown.

However, fishing is what the island is famous for and this has been so for centuries.

There is an 18th-century painting in the National Museum in Seoul that portrays a rudimentary fishing method, a sort of stone en-

closure standing in the water, identical to the method still used today on the island of Namhae. The island is connected by a bridge to the south coast of the Korean peninsula, the part of the country where anchovy fishing thrives and the coast is broken up into myriad archipelagos. Most of these have been declared a National Maritime Park by the Korean government.

In the tiny village of Jijuk-ri on the north side of the island, the celebrated anchovies of Namhae have for centuries been caught using a unique method called jukbang, literally 'bamboo nets'. The same term is used to indicate the catch, the much appreciated jukbang anchovies. There is mention of this delicacy as early as 1650, when census officials from the registrar's office of the Yi dynasty (1390 – 1910) noted that jukbang fishing was one of the most flourishing activities in the islands of this region. The waters here are clean. There are no factories to discharge effluents. Nor is there any significant maritime traffic, or the tourism typical of European coasts.

The village of Jijuk-ri looks onto a narrow stretch of sea, the strip of water that separates the two green landmasses connected by the Changseongyo steel bridge to form the island of Namhae. The water in the strait rushes in and out twice a day over a dis-tance of 12 kilometers and the tides between May and November lower the water level considerably. Early in the morning and in the evening, the water is about three meters deep, as opposed to five or six at high tide. The fish swim in muddy, nutrient-rich water, which is ideal for their healthy growth. The mud, the water and the tides, together with the local climate, are the environmental factors that explain why it is here and not elsewhere that anchovy fishing has been able to flourish over the centuries, attaining unassailable levels of quality.

**The enclosures in the water**

In the strip of sea that washes against the houses of Jijuk-ri, you can see the close-packed juk-bang. At first glance, they look like fences, with poles emerging from the water like the teeth of a comb. Seen from above, each of them resembles a truncated upside-down 'V', with an 'O' on top. The base of the upside-down V has a width varying from 30 to 50 meters and is open to the current, while the 'neck' narrows down to five meters, and in some cases to only one. The O, which has a diameter of four or five meters, is the area where the anchovies are collected, driven by the flow of water through the narrowing in the neck. The entire structure of a jukbang comprises 300 to 400 oak poles (though iron ones are now also being used), each ten meters high with a diameter of around 30 centimeters. The poles are driven into the sandy seabed about 60 centimeters apart, marking off the shape of the jukbang.

A tightly packed curtain of bamboo canes, two or three centimeters thick and four meters high, is positioned in the spaces between the oak poles. The canes are bound to each other with nylon line to form a bamboo 'sieve' running around the entire structure. This is in turn covered by fishing net with a one and a half-centimeter square mesh. The system thus only selects fish of a certain minimum size, allowing smaller ones to pass through the net and canes. All the larger fish are driven into the O by the strength of the current.

The circular area of the structure can be accessed via a small one-meter opening at boat height. It is filled with gravel at the beginning of the season to make it shallower and enable the fisherman to walk on the gravel bed. He can then catch the fish in small nets at the twice-daily low tide. The O is cleaned out every day before it is fished so that the water has no waste and the anchovies can swim in an environment free of impurities. The fish are loaded live onto the boat, put into plastic containers filled with brine, and then quickly taken to the fisher-

man's processing area, a hut on the beach. There the anchovies are tossed into a large pan of boiling water on an open fire and boiled – 110 seconds for the larger fish, 90 seconds for the others. They are then laid out to dry on shelves made of long bamboo canes. The whole process, including the journey, may be repeated five or six times if the fishing is good. The anchovies are thrown into a pan of boiling water only a few minutes after they are caught: this short time lapse constitutes one of the trump cards of jukbang fishing and accounts for the unbeatable freshness of the product. When the O has been completely emptied and all the anchovies have dried off on the bamboo canes, it is time for intensive drying. The anchovies are placed all along the jetty in shallow wicker-baskets to dry in the sun and salty wind from the sea. During periods of bad weather, drying is carried out artificially using special dehumidifiers and it is this process that enables the anchovies to remain crisp and flavorsome for up to a year, if kept in a refrigerator. Jukbang anchovies, caught and prepared with a simple, natural method that is both efficient and unique, are at this point ready to be canned and sold. Supply is very limited and demand is high, so prices are robust. Koreans eat anchovies in all sorts of ways, in-

cluding raw in sashimi, marinated, fried, salted and smoked, but the most popular version is dried anchovies, which are served as appetizers with alcoholic drinks. The fishermen give the anchovies various names, according to size. The smallest are sirengi, slightly larger ones are called kojuba and then come the honjuba, which are the most highly regarded of all.

Value does not always correspond to size, however. The next size up, the largest of all, is ojuba, which are the least valuable and make up the ten percent of the jukbang catch that is not dried. These are the so-called 'wet anchovies', which are considerably less valuable.

May and June are the best months for jukbang fishing, which is suspended from December to April. The price of a two-kilogram pack of kojuba can reach the equivalent of USD 100 and on average, the price of jukbang anchovies is four times higher than that of the industrial catch.

Their quality is primarily due to freshness. Anchovies caught by large vessels using huge nets undergo a series of detrimental intermediate processing stages during which the heads may be cut, the skin damaged or the guts ripped open. In contrast, jukbang anchovies swim in clean mineral-rich waters until just before they are the last moment, remaining healthy and full of flavor. Photographs of anchovies are prominently displayed in every Namhae tourist brochures, as well as in the pictures that hang in local authority offices on the island. The reputation is so high that supplies quickly sell out but nobody in the village has any intention of boosting production to increase profits.

## One family, one jukbang

There are 23 jukbangs altogether on Namhae. In the whole of Korea, this age-old method of fishing is now only carried out here and on the island of Samchonpo, where the water is not so pure and the anchovies not so highly prized. If you want to buy the best jukbang on Namhae today, it would cost the equivalent of around USD 200,000, while the least expensive would be worth around USD 40,000. The significant difference in values, a sign of economic health, is mainly determined by the jukbang's location since it is the currents that decide catch that each jukbang will ensure over the year. On average, the catch for each jukbang is about 3,000 kilograms in poor years and 9,000 kilograms if things go well. The total annual production of the village is 252 tons.

During the off-season, some fisherman grow garlic but most spend their time in these months mending their nets, repairing their boat, and, particularly, painstakingly making new bamboo screens, which have to be replaced every year. Each jukbang belongs to one family with just one, the most productive, owned jointly by two partners. The entire population of the village of Jijuk-ri, 24 families in all, is involved in anchovy fishing. By tradition, husband and wife work together, spending the entire day in the water, in the boat and in the store. Sometimes, the older sons help their parents with the work but the girls are not allowed to help until they are married. There is absolutely no question of small children being involved in fishing, which is an indication of civilized working conditions.

There is no official organization in the village representing the jukbang fishermen, just a social club. There is no competition or rivalry, everyone respects everybody else and each fishing family looks after his own business. The fishermen have enough to enjoy a decent standard of living and some young people from the village have gone to university. What binds this small fishing community together is a dignity and pride that are immediately discernible in every individual. These qualities come from the conviction that their product is of unbeatable quality and that they belong to a unique tradition, acknowledged and appreciated by the Yi dynasty, Korea's most prestigious royal house.

Rew Kuang Choon has no official position within the community but his quiet charisma, his pride and authority have gained him the re-spect of the whole village. The fisherfolk of Jijuk-ri have always supported in his defense of a tradition that, above all else, means identity.

*Stefano Sardo*

**Motives for Slow Food Award**

Rew Kuang Choon and the small fishing community of Jijuk-ri village are a fine example of an economy alternative to that of the standardizing forces of the global market. At Jijuk-ri, work is on a family scale, competition is interpreted in a non-aggressive way and the productive process is environmentally sustainable. The fishing community has managed to save an ancient way of life and a unique product by focusing naturally on quality. This is not a piece of the past which refuses to die, nor is it a quaint tradition put on for the benefit of tourists. If jukbang fishing continues, it is primarily because it is still commercially viable. Its competitiveness has been assured over time by the excellence of the product itself. The quality of jukbang anchovies has been maintained because the community has conserved the necessary conditions: freshness, hygiene, authenticity, environmental friendliness and moderate production levels.

The key factor is love for the product. That love brings a sense of dignity and pride which Rew Kuang Choon embodies in an exemplary fashion. The fisherfolk of Jijuk-ri are not looking for money or aid but instead seek the respect due to anyone who works well. An international prize such as the Slow Food Award may provide an extra stimulus to the younger generation to keep alive this minor but emblematic tradition.

## Slow Food Worldwide

The new year opens on a high note for the international Slow Food movement, which today has 70,000 members, half of them in **Italy** - where there has been significant growth after the launch of the Master of Food project, discussed elsewhere in this newsletter - and the other half mostly in the US, Germany, Switzerland, France, Great Britain, Japan, the Benelux countries, Austria and Australia.

Vincent Schiavelli, one of the characters in the film *Ghost*; the opening of several new convivia is planned over the next few months in California (**San Diego**, **San Luis Obispo**, **Lake Tahoe**), New York State (**Albany** and **Hudson Valley**), Oregon (**Eugene**), Iowa (**Des Moines**) and, for the first time, Kentucky (**Lexington**) and **Maine**. The enthusiasm and momentum of the movement in the US should be sufficient to achieve the objectives of 15,000 members

the last two years. In December 2001, the number of card-carrying members neared 7,000 and numerous new convivia - including **Achern-Ortenau**, **Bamberg**, **Erzgebirge-Vogtland**, **Mosel**, **Odenwald** and **Schwäbisch-Gmünd -** opened their doors. A full program of activities is documented in detail in the new German newsletter, edited by Manfred Kriener. The most successful event in 2001 was the *Slow Food Festival* in Bonn. Aside from a lovely show-

*By Elena Marino*

News comes from the **United States** of the recent transfer of our offices to the elegant headquarters of the French Culinary Institute, in the SoHo neighborhood of Manhattan. This has enabled us to expand our staff and expand activities. The number of American members has now reached 7,000 and over the past few months, new convivia have been started in **Hawaii, Pennsylvania** and **Houston**; the convivium in **Hollywood**, whose co-fiduciary is actor

before the end of 2002, and the opening of at least one convivium in each of the 50 states. Finally, among the new items in the new year, planning has started for the first *Slow Food Day*, a day for promoting nationwide the Ark project, the first American Presidia and Taste Education programs in schools.

**Germany** also began the new year with a positive growth trend, considerably higher with respect to

case of German and Italian agricultural and food products, the Festival also presented a program of more than 30 Taste Workshops and a Taste Education Course for children that was received with great interest. Slow Food Germany will be ten years old in 2002. The occasion will be celebrated during the Congress of German Members planned for May in Munich.

**Switzerland** has held onto its fourth place the membership stakes, reaching 3,000 in December 2001. This is partly due to the success of numerous projects, some of international importance. Among these, we mention *Super-Whites*, the wine fair held in Zurich at the end of November that offered two days of great white wines from Friuli, along with both Italian and Swiss food and drink, from salamis to cheeses, bread to potatoes, and coffee to grappas. *SuperWhites* was also the occasion for the official launch of the Swiss Ark project,

ther convivia were recently inaugurated: **Waldviertel**, in Wachau - an important wine-grape growing area, especially known for its whites - and **Nordburgerland**, one of Austria's finest winemaking territories, which produces superb, late-harvest, dried-grape wines.

In **France**, growth of the movement has been slower but the association has signed up its 1,500th member. Last year was important since it saw the move-

volved in celebrating this characteristic variety from the south of France and the Spanish coast. During 2002, many French convivia will be involved in the AMA Ferme project, a partnership between farmers and consumers in which the latter prepay a farm for produce that will be delivered to them on a weekly basis. Created along the lines of a similar project launched in the US and Canada, this initiative immediately gained the support of Slow Food

# world

in which Slow Food Pays de Romandie, Slow Food German Switzerland and Slow Food Ticino will participate, and the nomination of an advisory committee to select the first Ark products. Assistance is coming from Pro Specie Rara, an association that has worked for the past two years to defend and promote threatened animal breeds and plant varieties.

In **Austria**, alongside the newly created group in Salzburg, two fur-

ment's participation for the first time at several internationally important events. In Bordeaux, at Vinexpo, Slow Food organized eight Taste Workshops matching great wines with food products from around the world, which met with success beyond all expectations. At Perpignan, the first *Journée Internationale du Grenache* was organized entirely by the convivia in the south of the country. Hundreds of wine producers and professionals were in-

Provence and will be extended to the whole country in 2002. Finally, an exhibition is being planned in Pau for 2002. It will be dedicated to cheeses from the Pyrenees, and attempts will be made to strengthen the presence of the association both through recently founded convivia in **Avignon** and **Saint-Etienne**, as well as the creation of new convivia at **Bordeaux** and **Lyon**, the city that will host the World Slow Food Congress in 2003.

Representatives from Slow Food International for the first time visited the convivia in **Japan** on the occasion of the *Italy in Japan* fair. This gave them the chance to experience first hand the great interest of Japan - particularly the capital - in our association and in issues of high quality production and the protection of the environment and biodiversity in general. Two new convivia were started in Tokyo and the number of members has tripled, reaching almost a thousand.

Snail in **Iceland**, **Lebanon**, **Venezuela**, **Chile** and **Yugoslavia**, along with Eastern Europe, particularly Russia and Poland, where the first convivia will be opened in the next few months.

## The Voyages of the Ark

The Ark of Taste is not just Italian. Slow Food convivia across the world are working to identify products to be saved, to set up advisory committees and define selection

identified methods and criteria for choosing products, similar to those applied in Italy. The first five products chosen for the German Ark are: the Finkenwerden Herbstprinz apple, a variety cultivated in northern Germany; the Angeliter Tannenzapfen potato grown in Schleswig-Holstein; Türksche Erbse, a kind of bean that is an essential ingredient in a famous boiled bacon dish from Schleswig-Holstein; pear cider from the Champagner Bratbirne

Interest in Slow Food has also noticeably grown in **Great Britain**. Today, the number of members has risen to almost a thousand, with major groups in **London**, **Manchester** and **Edinburgh**. New publishing projects are planned for 2002, including the translation of several Slow Food publications into English to give greater visibility to the movement.

Finally, we would also like to mention the leisurely inroads of our

criteria. Though some of the five Italian criteria can be exported – and the first, gastronomic excellence, must be a discriminating factor in evaluating products anywhere in the world – there will naturally be local adjustments and corrections for each individual country. For example, historic connection with the territory has different meanings in Europe, America or Australia.

In **Germany**, an Ark committee has drawn up a manifesto and

variety; and the Bavarian turnip. Furthermore, an important research project was begun in the summer of 2001, financed by the regional council office for agricultural policy of North Rhine-Westphalia. Information brochures on the Ark project were printed and distributed across the region along with cards marked 'Ark boarding card application'. As work proceeds, a website will list other products to be saved. For further information, contact Slow Food Deutschland, Münster: tel. + + 49

(0) 251 793368; e-mail: <u>info@slow-food.de</u>.

Running the Ark of Taste in **France** is Didier Chabrol, president of the Languedoc convivium. An advisory committee of agronomists, botanists, ethnologists, food and agricultural technologists, historians and journalists constantly selects products to be listed, including the Duclair goose, the Loire salmon, Pied Bleu mushrooms, Chiche de Carlencas peas, and so

for gastronomic excellence and an initial list of Ark products will soon be available.

In **Great Britain** and **Austria**, the local Slow Food associations are also setting up Ark committees and the convivia have begun to select the first products, including Herdwick sheep from the Lake District and Pinzgauer cattle from the Salzburg region.

In **Australia**, the first Slow Food

mail: <u>lfurber@ozemail.com.au</u>).

In the **United States**, the vast extent of the territory and the huge differences from one region to another prompted the Ark Committee, presided over by Slow Food governor Barbara Bowman (Msbrix@aol.com), has been organized into eight macroregional areas, each with its own director. All local groups must send recommendations to their respective regional representatives: Barbara Bowman

*Slow Food Award, Oporto*

on). For further information, contact Didier Chabrol: tel. + + 33 4 67 04 75 86; e-mail: <u>chabrol@agropolis.fr</u>.

In **Switzerland**, the local group has appointed a committee that will select the first products and make contact with local environmental groups defending and promoting individual products, vegetable varieties and animal breeds that are threatened with extinction. The local convivia have started identifying the most interesting products

conference held in Melbourne in August 1999 defined areas of Ark activity, including products from Aboriginal culture to those of the early colonies and others introduced more recently. Slow Food is being organized into regional work groups that will draw up criteria for the Australian Ark. For further information, contact James Broadway (tel. + + 61 394890930 - + + 61 395340414; e-mail: ajbroadway@hotmail.com) or Leonie Furber (tel. + + 61 293808327 - + + 61 418267499; e-

for the Western region; Deborah Madison, Southwest (deborah-madison@earthlink.net); Gerry Warren, Northwest (gwarren@u.washington.edu); Tami Lax, Midwest (tami@harvest-restaurant.com); Poppy Tooker, South (poppyt@bell-south.net); Jeff Roberts, North East (cowcreek@attglobal.net). Representatives will also be nominated in the next few months for the Rocky Mountain and Atlantic States.
The requirements laid down by the Ark Committee for products identi-

fied by the groups are largely similar to those in Italy, with the exception of the requirement of a long acclimitazation period for the animal and vegetable varieties. This is impractical in a situation that is still very dynamic and striving to achieve maximum gastronomic potential from local production. We particularly mention the campaign to defend several rare species of turkey, including the American Bronze, the Bourbon Red, the Jersey Buff and the Narragansett.

that risks being lost and to spread the awareness of production and tasting techniques, along with the history and culture of food, wine and gastronomy. All this in addition to encouraging an approach to food that is aware yet convivial, informed and pleasant.

All across Italy, **courses** are being held on: beer; coffee, teas and infusions; meats; cereals, pasta, bread; sweets, chocolate, honey and fruit preserves; cheeses; distilled and alcohol based products; oil; fruits

transmission of this knowledge, which is spontaneous and almost automatic in rural, farming cultures, is one of the requirements necessary to re-establish civilized ways of living together. Increasing ignorance on the subject of food leaves room for exploitation by the unscrupulous and does not help the recovery of agriculture. Without the well-rooted conviction that food education is as indispensable as knowing how to read and write, it is impossible to plan the development

Thanks to the work carried out over the last few months by the national office, this project presently brings together 15 producers in 11 states.

**Master of Food**

In 2002, Slow Food Italia will be starting the Master of Food, the great teaching project for food, wine and sensory qualities, designed to be a genuine, open-access University of Taste. The aim is to recover taste-related knowledge

and vegetables; fish; salami and preserved meats; food science and technology; spices, aromas and vinegar; the history and culture of gastronomy; cooking techniques; wine; and world food. The courses comprise from three to six classes and present the Slow Food philosophy and style. In other words, rather than an exclusively academic in design, they strike a balance between scientific content and an appealing teaching style.

Slow Food is convinced that the

of clean resources, and defend biodiversity and gastronomic heritage. The Master of Food format will be reproduced in all those countries where the movement is present and will be the guiding idea for Slow Food's cultural policy. On the one hand, this is to support new agriculture and, on the other, to develop an education project underpinning the historic alliance between production and consumption. The ultimate objective of the Master of Food is to reinforce new trends in consumption.

If there is in the next few years a wider knowledge of cheesemaking, of indigenous livestock, of working with yeasts in bread and wine, of the art of making hams and salami, of clean biotechnology and organic farming, then a new generation of educated, curious and aware consumers will have been born.

## Slow Food Book

Chelsea Green Publishing Company, a publishing house in Vermont and closes with the cuisine of leftovers, covering in between a huge range subjects that fully reflect the wealth of contributions, reflections and stimulating ideas that *Slow* has delivered over the past few years, both to the movement and the whole world. Traditions and street foods, beer and markets, taboos and biotechnologies, wine and meat: these are just a few of the themes on which the book hinges. There are also some thoughts about what the Skimming over the table of contents, we are amazed at this ability to produce a truly cultural magazine, capable of hosting contributions with starkly different inspirations but all with the same, strictly Slow Food, objective: to reflect on natural diversity and the richness that comes from it. In short, this volume by Chelsea Green brings back the sense and originality of a very special, culturally significant, publishing experience.

# world

specializing in environment-related publications, has just sent to press *Slow Food – Collected Thoughts on Taste, Tradition, and the Honest Pleasures of Food.* It's is a collection of around 70 articles that have appeared in *Slow* magazine over the past six years, 1994 to 2000. The articles, with a preface by Deborah Madison and introductions by Carlo Petrini and Patrick Martins, are arranged into 15 chapters by topic. The book opens with reflections on the Ark publication has attempted to do, and what it has actually accomplished, over the past few years. Most impressive of all is the ability of *Slow* to anticipate issues that would later quickly become news, on occasion dramatic. We recall the reports on intensive livestock-raising techniques and related risks, published long before the hullabaloo over mad cow disease. Or the articles on biotechnologies, anticipating a debate that would later be very significant.

*Slow Food*
*Collected Thoughts on Taste, Tradition, and the Honest Pleasures of Food*
Chelsea Green Publishing Company
USD 24.95

**Slow Food Calendar 2002**

### From 20 to 24 February – Medial at Palermo

At Medial, the *Fiera del Mediterraneo Alimentare* (Mediterranean Food Fair) in Palermo, Slow Food Italia will be presenting the Sicilian Presidia, both those already established as well as the new ones that will be officially inaugurated at the event.

guage edition of the *Osterie d'Italia* restaurant guide, published by Hallwag, is scheduled to take place in March.

### From 18 to 21 April – Slow Food on Film at Bra

The first international festival of short films entirely dedicated to the love of food will be held in April at Bra, as part of the fourth edition of the *Festival Cinema Corto in Bra* (Bra Short Film Festival), organized by the municipality of Bra in collaboration with Slow Food.

pate in *Vinitaly*, the prestigious Verona wine fair, now in its 36th edition. Among the various initiatives planned are food and wine conferences, tastings and international events.

### April and May – The English editions of *Vini d'Italia* and *Osterie d'Italia*

The English-language edition of the *Vini d'Italia* wine guide will be in bookstores in April and the *Osterie d'Italia* restaurant guide will be out in May.

### 18 February – Presentation of the German edition of *Vini d'Italia*

The German language edition of the *Vini d'Italia 2002* wine guide will be presented in Munich at the Aktionsforum Praterinsel exhibition center on 18 February at 1 pm. It will be followed by a tasting of Three Glass wines, open to the press, wine professionals and the public.

### March – The German edition of *Osterie d'Italia*

The presentation of the German-lan-

The president of the jury will be celebrated Hollywood character actor, Vincent Schiavelli, also the author of several cookbooks and co-fiduciary of the Slow Food convivium in Los Angeles. The closing date for entries is 31 January 2002. Films in competition will also be presented online at the international site of the Snail, www.slowfood.com.

### From 11 to 15 April – Vinitaly at Verona

Again this year, Slow Food will partici-

### Late April – SuperWhites in New York

Now in its third edition, this classic showcase for the white wines of Friuli and American food products will be held at the end of April in the Puck Building. The event will include a full schedule of food and wine events and Taste Workshops.

### May – Barbecue Pig Fest at Brooklyn

After the success of the 2001 edition,

Slow Food USA will be repeating the *Barbecue Pig Fest* to be held at the Brooklyn Brewery. A unique opportunity to savor products made with meat from animals raised using sustainable agricultural methods.

**April – Presentation of the *Atlante dei prodotti tipici e tradizionali del Sistema Nazionale delle Aree Protette* (Atlas of Typical and Traditional Products from the National**

dresses of producers operating in protected areas.

**From 3 to 5 May – Congress of German Slow Food members at Munich**

Slow Food Germany will celebrate its tenth birthday in 2002 during the Congress of German members to be held from 3 to 5 May in Munich.

**26 May - *Northern Cheeses* at Hamburg**

winelovers in a celebration of this grape variety native to the south of France and the Spanish coast.

**June – National Congress of Slow Food Italia**

Planned for the month of June, this assembly will elect the various governing bodies and officers of the Italian movement.

**June-July – International Governors' Meeting**

**System of Protected Areas)**
The *2a Conferenza Nazionale Aree Naturali Protette* (Second National Conference of Protected Natural Areas) will feature a presentation of this publishing initiative by Slow Food, in collaboration with Legambiente and Federparchi, promoted by the Italian Ministry of the Environment. It is a map of all the typical, traditional products – from oils to wines, bread and cheeses – made in 19 National Parks and 70 Regional Parks, along with the ad-

For the fourth year, Slow Food Germany is presenting the cheese exhibition, *Northern Cheeses*, to be held at the end of May in Hamburg.

**May – Journée Internationale du Grenache at Châteauneuf-du-Pape**
The second edition of the *Journée Internationale du Grenache* will be held in Châteauneuf-du-Pape. The event, organized by Slow Food France, will involve producers, professionals and

The exact date is still to be decided for the annual international meeting of Slow Food Governors, whose main business will be planning the 2003 International Congress and the revision of the Statute.

**From 30 August to 1 September 1 – *German Cheese Market* at Nieheim**
Nieheim will host the third edition of the *German Cheese Market*, a food fair organized in collaboration with

Slow Food Germany. It will offer an opportunity to taste the products of more than 80 local craft cheesemakers and to participate in numerous Taste Workshops.

### 23 October at Turin – Slow Food Award

After Bologna and Oporto, Turin is next to host the third edition of the Slow Food Award, an international recognition given to those who have worked in the defense of biodiversity.

### From October 24 to 28: the *Salone del Gusto* at Turin

The fourth edition of the *Salone del Gusto* (Hall of Taste) will be held at the Lingotto conference center in Turin. This well-established, and much-anticipated, event is organized by Slow Food, in conjunction with the Piedmont regional authority. More than a mere trade fair, the *Salone del Gusto* is major cultural event in the food and wine sector, and the most important on the international scene.

Central themes for 2002 will be taste education and the defense of biodiversity.

**The Slow Food Calendar will be updated in the following editions of this publication. It is also constantly updated in the English section of our website, www.slowfood.it, in the *Grandi Eventi* (Major Events) section of the Slow Calendar.**